First published 2023. Not for resale.

ISBN: 9798872009061
Imprint: Independently published

Photographers:
Front cover photo and page 11 - Travis Ball
London - Ashley kelleher
Hossegor section - James Sweet @superradness
Mount Everest Photos - Christian Debney
Other Food photography - Nick Pumphrey & Dave White
Norway - Kene E-O

Published by Dave White.

Designed by Design & Nurture.

More on instagram.com/chefdavewhite

# SALTED

## CHEF DAVE WHITE

*Cooking saved my life*

A RECIPE BOOK WITH A STORY TO TELL

Within these pages are 50 recipes acquired throughout my travels around the world and my adventures along the way. Whether at home or on the road, on yachts or mountain tops, I personally created and photographed every dish. Included are also some incredible pictures from talented friends whose contributions to this book and to my life I'm grateful for. It was important to me while creating these recipes that no professional equipment or experience be required. These meals are meant to be shared wherever you are with whomever you love. I hope it'll help you find inspiration anywhere life takes you - in the kitchen and beyond.

This book is a window into the worlds that saved me.

I want to share my story, and have realized that this journey is not one of shame, embarrassment or weakness, but one of strength. I hope in doing so that I help others find their strength too.

This book is dedicated to all of those who struggle with their mental health, and to anyone who feels alone or lost along the way as I've been myself.

To my family who reminded me I deserved the world even when I couldn't see it. Mum, you taught me empathy and to wear my heart on my sleeve. To my brothers who gave me the strength I have today and my sister who gives me hope. Dad, your wisdom and work ethic are why I never let my foot off the gas on my path to becoming a chef. To my friends – you welcomed me when I was lost and gave me a second chance. You know who you are and I'm forever grateful.

The passion I have in the kitchen is matched by my love for adrenaline and adventure. To keep my body busy is to keep my demons quiet. To push the boundaries in nature allows me to push my boundaries as a chef, and inspiration is always ready to be discovered when you open yourself up to the world.

For these reasons, I'll be climbing Mt. Everest to raise awareness for mental health and to inspire others to see that what you think is impossible is possible. But that's a story for another time.

For now, I hope you'll enjoy this compilation of simple, beloved recipes from my travels around the world and a glimpse into the accompanying adventures beyond the kitchen.

With Love,

*Chef Dave White*

# CONTENTS

# ENGLAND

## ALONG THE COAST AND IN THE CITY

I was born with a fighting spirit, but growing up I channeled it in all the wrong ways. My father had me start washing dishes at a local restaurant in the hopes I'd stay out of trouble. In the years that followed, I'd alternate between the kitchen and jail cells, struggling to control my emotions even as I gained control of my skills as a chef. Despite graduating to work in Michelin Star restaurants in London, I knew I needed to change my surroundings and allow myself a fresh start, so I decided to take a gamble and wow, was I scared.

# FISH N CHIPS

## WITH TARTAR SAUCE

Serves 4

## INGREDIENTS

**4 fillets of white fish (ask the fish monger to pin bone and skin)**

**3 cups all purpose flour**

**1 tsp baking powder**

**1 tsp baking soda**

**2 cups of cold soda water**

**8 large clean potatoes**

**1 cup all purpose flour for dusting**

**1 tbsp cider vinegar**

### TARTAR SAUCE

**1 whole egg**

**1 lemon juiced**

**1 cup olive oil**

**1 tbsp chopped parsley**

**1 tbsp finely diced gherkins**

**1 tbsp small capers (don't chop)**

### FOR SEASONING

**Lemon**

**Malt vinegar**

**Salt**

## METHOD

Very cold meeting very hot is what will create a reaction. When battered lightly, you can still taste the beautifully flaky fish but with a tender crisp. Texture is heaven - no one wants soggy or dry fish!

Ideally use cod, pollock, haddock or hake. Pin bone and skin the fish. Salt well and place in the fridge. Do not cover as we want to dry the fish out for at least an hour to withdraw the moisture and tenderize the fish.

For the tartar sauce put the oil, lemon juice, tsp of salt and raw egg in a jug and use a stick blender to mix until it emulsifies. Fold in the capers, gherkins and chopped parsley and then place in the fridge.

Put on a large pot of water with a tbsp of salt and cider vinegar and bring to a boil. Cut the chips to your desired size, ideally 0.5 cm a square, then blanch for 10minutes. Take out and place on a clean towel.

Use a fryer or put on a large pot with sunflower oil and bring it to 400°F/200°C. The amount of oil depends on your pot but the deeper the better. Now, fry the chips one handle at a time. Repeat 3 times; triple fried gives you the best finish. You might even want to flash your chips once more before serving, after the fish is done.

For the batter, add the flour, salt, baking powder, and baking soda into a bowl. Pour in the fizzy cold water to form a paste. Continue to add until you have a cream-like consistency. Add ice cubes and place in the fridge.

Bring the oil back to at least 400°F/200°C.

Remove the fish from the fridge and wipe the salt away with a paper towel. The salt acts as a quick cure. Then roll in flour and dip in the ice-cold batter before gently placing into the oil. After 2 minutes remove onto a paper towel. Important: you must fry one at a time to keep the oil hot.

Once you have your 4 pieces partly cooked wait for the oil to reheat above 400°F/200°C as this will also allow for the excess water to escape – also known as resting. Then go one by one for another 2 minutes. This final flash will give you your perfect finish! Season with malt vinegar, lemon and salt.

*Chef's Note*

There is gluten free flour by King Arthur called Measure For Measure that works just as well, if not better, just add soda water to it to provide the same finish. Honestly, it's a great alternative!

# YORKSHIRE PUDDING

Serves 12

## INGREDIENTS

1 ½ cups all-purpose flour

¾ teaspoon salt

¾ cup milk, room temperature

3 large eggs, room temperature

¾ cup water

## METHOD

Mix together flour and salt in a large bowl and form a well in the center. Add milk and whisk until combined. Beat in eggs until incorporated. Add water and beat until mixture is light and frothy. Cover and set aside at room temperature for 1 hour (or if it's the day before, store covered in the refrigerator for 8 hours to overnight).

Preheat the oven to 400°F/200°C.

Pour sunflower oil into a non-stick muffin tray and place in the preheated oven until oil is piping hot. Pour batter evenly over hot oil using all the mix and bake until the sides have risen and turned golden brown, about 30 minutes.

# TOAD IN THE HOLE

Serves 6

## INGREDIENTS

**2 red onions sliced**

**12 thick cumberland sausages**

FOR THE BATTER

**1 ½ cups all-purpose flour**

**¾ teaspoon salt**

**¾ cup milk, room temperature**

**3 large eggs, room temperature**

**¾ cup water**

## METHOD

Heat the oven to 400°F/200°C. Put the sausages in a 20x30cm roasting tin with the oil and onions and bake for 15 mins until browned.

Make the batter, follow the Yorkshire pudding recipe on the page prior to this.

Remove the sausages from the oven – be careful because the fat will be sizzling hot – but if it isn't, put the tin on the hob for a few minutes until it is.

Pour in the batter mix, transfer to the top shelf of the oven, then cook for 25-30 mins, until risen and golden. Serve with onion gravy and your favourite veg.

# PORK AND THYME SAUSAGE ROLLS

Serves 8

## INGREDIENTS

30g/1oz butter

2 peeled finely diced apples

1 tbsp whole grain mustard

1 tbsp Worcestershire sauce

1 tbsp Tabasco sauce

1 tbsp dried thyme

450g/1lb sausage meat

Salt

Freshly ground black pepper

450g/1lb ready-rolled puff pastry

1 free-range egg, beaten

## METHOD

Preheat the oven to 400°F/200°C.

Add the Worcestershire sauce, apple, whole grain mustard, Tabasco sauce, thyme and sausage meat and season well with salt and freshly ground black pepper. Mix until thoroughly combined.

Roll the puff pastry out into a large rectangle, then cut into two long rectangles.

Place a layer of sausage meat mixture down the middle of each pastry rectangle, then brush with beaten egg on one of the long edge.

Fold the other side of the pastry over onto the egg-washed edge. Press down to seal and trim any excess. Cut each pastry roll into 8-10 small sausage rolls.

Place the sausage rolls onto a baking tray and bake for 15-20 minutes, or until the pastry is crisp and golden and the sausage meat is completely cooked through.

# CORNISH PASTIE

Serves 6

*In my opinion, the Cornish pastie is probably the best thing to come out of England. This D-shaped pastry is packed full of flavor. Traditionally it's made with short crust pastry, but honestly I prefer mine with puff. While much more skill is needed to make puff pastry, you can just buy it from your local supermarket!*

## INGREDIENTS

500g (17.6oz) ready made puff pastry or home made short crust

500g (17.6oz) all purpose flour

125g (4.4oz) lard, cold and diced

125g (4.4oz) unsalted butter, cold and diced

400g (14.1oz) ground short rib

200g (7.1oz) potatoes, diced

150g (5.3oz) turnip, diced

150g (5.3oz) onion, diced

Small bunch thyme, finely slice

1 egg, beaten

Salt and pepper

## METHOD

Add the flour, butter, lard, and a big pinch of salt to a food processor and process until the fat is well incorporated.

Next, with the processor still running, pour in around 150ml of ice-cold water. Start with 100ml and keep adding little by little until the dough comes together. Turn this out onto a clean surface and bring it together with your hands. Wrap it in cling film and refrigerate for 30 minutes.

To make the filling, simply add the beef, potato, swede, onions, and thyme to a bowl. Season with salt and pepper and mix well.

Preheat the oven to 180°C (356°F) and then roll out the dough, aiming for the dough to be 30-40mm thick. Using something round, cut out disks of the pastry. Place the filling into one half of a disk of pastry and then fold the other side over, crimp the edges well, and then place onto a lightly greased oven tray.

Pop 3 small holes in the top of each one, then brush with the egg wash, and bake in the oven at 180°C (356°F) for 45 minutes.

Let them rest for at least 15 minutes after you take them out of the oven because these things are super hot.

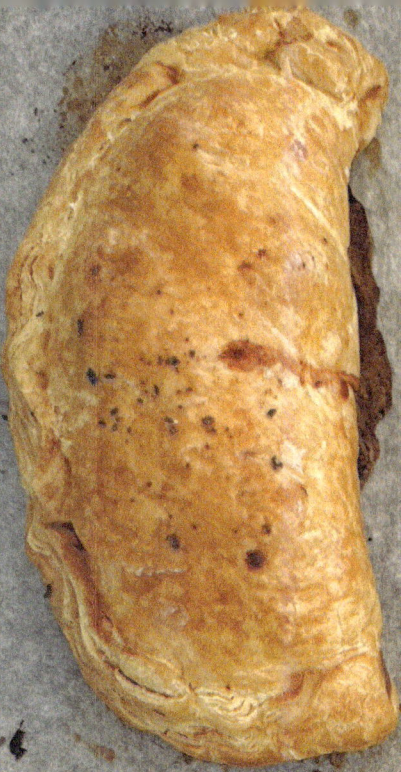

# 5 MINUTE SWEET PEA AND GARLIC SOUP

## WITH FRESH MINT LEAVES

Serves 6

*This one is souper, trust me! Peas are a good source of vitamins C and E, zinc, and other antioxidants that strengthen your immune system and help reduce inflammation. The easiest soup to do in minimal time, the bright green color and sweet pea flavor is just to die for. I could tell you to make a Mirepoix but honestly, there really is no need. Peas are packed full of flavor and keeping it simple is best.*

### INGREDIENTS

**2 cups of defrosted frozen peas**

**4 cups of chicken stock**

**Fresh mint sprigs**

**2 cloves of garlic diced**

**2 tbsp olive oil**

**Salt and ground white pepper**

### METHOD

Bring your stock to a boil with the garlic cloves and simmer for 2 minutes – this will take the punch out of the garlic.

Put the peas in a blender, ideally a Vitamix or Nutribullet as they make the best purées. Pour in the stock and garlic, add salt to taste but only a small pinch of white pepper, along with 3 tablespoons of olive oil and blend until smooth.

Add to a pot and bring up to your desired temperature but don't boil it, and watch that beautiful green come alive! I like to blend it once more to get a real velouté finish. Before you serve add some fresh mint and a little dollop of sour cream and black pepper. This is a perfect dish to serve with a wrap or a sandwich.

*Chef's Note*

The key is to not overheat the peas!

# BEEF SCOTCHED EGG WITH DIJONNAISE

Serves 6

## INGREDIENTS

6 eggs

1 apple peeled and diced apple

1 tbsp chopped parsley

1 tbsp horseradish

1 diced shallot

1lb ground beef short rib

1 cup flour

2 cups fine bread crumbs

Sunflower oil for frying

Salt and pepper

### DIJONNAISE

1 cup of mayonnaise

1 tbsp Dijon mustard

1 juiced lemon

## METHOD

Bring a pan of salted water to a rapid boil, then lower 4 of the eggs into the pan and simmer for 7 minutes exactly. Scoop out and place in a bowl of iced water, cracking the shells a little (this makes them easier to peel later). Leave them to cool completely, then peel and set aside.

Combine the apple, shallot, parsley, and horseradish and then divide into four equal balls. Squash one of the balls between a piece of cling film until it's as flat as possible. Use the cling film to help roll the sausage meat around the egg to completely encase. Repeat with the remaining beef balls and eggs, and then place in the freezer for 30 minutes. This will make it easier to work with and keep the yolk runny.

Beat the remaining 2 eggs and put on a plate. Put the flour and breadcrumbs on two separate plates. Roll the encased eggs in the flour, then the beaten egg and finally the breadcrumbs. These can be prepared up to a day in advance.

To cook the eggs, heat 5cm of the oil in a wide saucepan or wok until it reaches 350°F/160°C. Depending on the size of your pan, lower as many eggs as you can into the oil and cook for 4 minutes until golden and crispy.

Place on a paper towel, and then cut them in half to appreciate the beautiful runny yolk and dip in your delicious Dijonnaise.

# WHITE CHOCOLATE AND RASPBERRY BREAD AND BUTTER PUDDING

## WITH CLOTTED CREAM

Serves 8

*A fantastic way to recycle old stale bread!*

## INGREDIENTS

2 cup of whole milk

1 cup double cream

1 tbsp vanilla extract

3 whole large eggs, plus 1 egg yolk

½ cup white sugar

16 slices stale bread

4oz soft salted butter

1 cup white chocolate drops

1 cup of fresh or frozen raspberries

4oz of light brown sugar

Clotted cream for garnish

1 Nutmeg grated

1 Lemon, zested

## METHOD

To make the custard, heat the milk, cream and vanilla pod (if using) with its scraped out seeds together in a saucepan to just below boiling point. Meanwhile whisk the eggs and yolk with the caster sugar in a bowl Slowly pour the warm milk mixture, including the vanilla pod, over the eggs, stirring constantly until smooth. If opting for the vanilla extract stir in now.

Lightly butter an ovenproof dish approximately 20cm x 25cm x 5cm. Cut the crusts from the bread slices, butter both sides of the bread and cut into triangles. Put the bread slices in the bottom of the dish so that they are slightly overlapping. Sprinkle in half of the raspberries and white chocolate over the bread. Layer the rest of the bread on top then sprinkle over the remaining berries and chocolate and repeat.

Heat oven to 400°F/200°C. Remove the vanilla pod from the custard then pour the custard over the pudding. Leave to soak for at least 30 minutes, or longer in the fridge, if you like. Sprinkle over the brown sugar and bake for 35-40 minutes until golden brown and puffed up.

Finish with clotted cream, a dusting of nutmeg and lemon zest.

*Chef's Note*

Use the crusts of the bread to make your own bread crumbs for the scotched egg on previous page.

# FRANCE

TIGNES FRENCH ALPS

I was 18 when I arrived in France, and it would be years before I'd understand how taking that leap saved me and changed the trajectory of my life.

I took  a sous chef position at a busy hotel. I was craving change and driven by ambition to become the best chef I could be. However, I was homesick and struggled with loneliness and dark thoughts. Seeking an outlet for these feelings, I tried skiing for the first time and discovered a talent and a passion I'm thankful to have found. In 2014, I claimed gold at the British Freestyle Skiing Championships. I still love to ski to this day, and love France for all that it's given me.

# CHORIZO FONDUE

Serves 4

*A traditional Savoyard dish with a twist, this is a delicious classic that can be made anywhere in minimal time. Whether on a stove, a grill, or on direct coals in the middle of nowhere at over 4000 meters elevation!*

## INGREDIENTS

1 shallot diced

2 cloves of garlic crushed

1 apple, peeled and diced

1 cup of diced chorizo

3 cups of grated Comte or Beaufort cheese

1 day old French baguette

Chefs pinch of salt

## METHOD

Pull apart your baguette into bite-size pieces. Do not cover as it should be stale.

Warm the pot and with the exception of the cheese, sauté all of your ingredients until caramelized and all the fat has come out of the chorizo. Now add the grated cheese. Don't stop stirring the contents as it will catch and burn. Remove from the heat once melted and add the salt.

Now dip that stale bread to your heart's content!

*Chef's Note*

Ideally, use a heavy, enameled metal pot made of cast iron. Because there is so much fat in the chorizo, this variation does not use the traditional wine. Instead, the delicious smoky oils from the chorizo are used to confit the cheese.

# CROQUE MONSIEUR WITH PULLED PORK

Serves 4

*This dish is traditionally done with ham, cheese, and béchamel sauce and then gratinated under the grill. My version is a croque monsieur on steroids.*

## INGREDIENTS

**Mornay sauce - see the next page**

**1lb pork shoulder**

**8 slices sliced sourdough bread**

**2 tbsp butter**

**2 tbsp Dijon mustard**

**1 cup of grated Parmesan**

**3 cups of lard or sunflower oil**

## METHOD

Roughly chop your pork up into four pieces and place in a heavy pot with your lard or sunflower oil on medium heat. Cover with foil and confit for 3 hours.

Remove the pork when tender onto a paper towel to drain the fat.
Pull apart the pork with hands or use a fork, then season with salt.
Put the pork back on and crisp it up, really helps with the texture.

Put a non-stick pan on medium heat. Spread a thick layer of butter on every side of the sourdough and caramelize the bread. Add a little olive oil to stop the butter from burning. Take out the pan and set aside.

Spread 1 tbsp of Dijon mustard and put a thick layer of pork on the bread with 2 tbsp of mornay sauce on top.

Place the slice on top with 3 tbsp of mornay sauce. Sprinkle 1 tbsp of Parmesan then gratinate using a blowtorch or under the grill.

# MORNAY SAUCE

## INGREDIENTS

**4 tbsp butter**

**⅓ cup all-purpose flour**

**3 cups whole milk, warm not hot**

**2 whole cloves**

**¼ medium onion, peeled**

**1 bay leaf**

**2oz grated Gruyère cheese**

**2oz grated Parmesan cheese**

## METHOD

In a heavy-bottomed saucepan, melt 3 tbsp of the butter over medium-low heat.

Stir in the flour to form a roux. Cook for 2 to 3 minutes, stirring frequently, until most of the water has cooked out (it will bubble less), which also allows the raw flour taste to cook off.

Slowly add 2 ½ cups of the warm milk while whisking or stirring constantly so that the liquid is incorporated into the roux without forming lumps.

Stick the cloves into the onion and add to the sauce along with the bay leaf. Simmer for about 10 minutes, or until it's reduced by about 20 percent.

Remove the bay leaf and the onion and strain the sauce through a fine-mesh strainer or a colander lined with cheesecloth. Make sure you retrieve all of the cloves.

Return the sauce to the pan. Add the Gruyère and Parmesan cheeses and stir until the cheese has melted.

Remove from heat and stir in the remaining 1 tbsp butter, and adjust the consistency with some or all of the remaining ½ cup milk if necessary. Serve immediately.

# TARTIFLETTE

Serves 8

## INGREDIENTS

**2lb  new potatoes**

**8oz bacon lardons**

**3 sliced shallots**

**2 garlic cloves sliced**

**½ cup white wine**

**1 cup double cream**

**Sea salt**

**Freshly ground black pepper**

**1lb Reblochon cheese, sliced**

**2 sprigs rosemary**

## METHOD

For the tartiflette, preheat oven to 400°F/200°C.

Cook the potatoes in a saucepan of salted boiling water for 5-10 minutes, or until tender. Drain and set aside to cool slightly, then peel with fingers.

Meanwhile, heat a frying pan until hot and sauté the bacon till rendered and crispy. Remove and put aside on paper towel.

Use the same pan to sauté the shallots, rosemary and garlic for 4-5 minutes, or until golden brown. Deglaze the pan with the white wine and continue to cook until most of the liquid has evaporated before adding the cream.

Slice the potatoes thinly - ideally on a mandolin at about 3mm each and layer into an ovenproof gratin dish with the creamy mixture, bacon and reblochon in between layers. Pour over the remaining mix at the end. Season with salt and plenty of freshly ground black pepper.

Layer the remaining reblochon slices on top and bake in the oven for 25 minutes or until the cheese is golden brown and bubbling.

# COCONUT MUSSELS

*It's hard to beat a Moules marinière but this is my favorite. Influenced by my time traveling in Asia, this fusion delicacy is delightful and so easy. It's a one-pot wonder! Just make sure your mussels are in season, which spans October to March. You will not be disappointed.*

## INGREDIENTS

**1 tbsp coconut oil**

**2 inch piece ginger sliced**

**2 shallots sliced**

**2 cloves of garlic sliced**

**2 stalks of lemongrass sliced**

**2 tins of light coconut milk**

**1 tsp fish sauce**

**2  green chilis, diced**

**2 tbsp of shredded coriander**

**Half a Chinese cabbage sliced**

**4 kafir lime leaves**

**2lb mussels rinsed and beards removed**

**Toasted coconut for garnish**

## METHOD

Heat the coconut oil in a large pot over medium-high heat. Add the ginger, garlic, shallots, kafir lime leaves, lemongrass and cook for 1 minute. Add the coconut milk, fish sauce, and bring the pot to a boil.

When the coconut milk is boiling, add the mussels. Cover the pot for 3 minutes, then add the cabbage.

If any of the mussels are still closed after 6 or 7 minutes, discard them. Throw in your fresh chilis and your coriander (including sliced stalks).

Remove your mussels and place in a bowl. Pour the sauce over the cooked mussels and serve right away. Finish with some toasted coconut.

# APPLE TARTE TATIN

Serves 6

*One of my favorite winter desserts! It's so easy to do and looks elegant on the plate. A banging one that takes little time, especially if your wanting to impress.*

INGREDIENTS

½ lb all-butter puff pastry

Plain flour for dusting

8 green apples

2 tbsp soft dark brown sugar

5oz unsalted butter (4oz chilled and diced, 1oz melted)

4 tbsp golden syrup

Cinnamon

Nutmeg

Ginger powder

METHOD

Roll the pastry to a 3mm-thick round on a lightly floured surface using a dinner plate as a guide. Lightly prick all over with a fork and place on a baking sheet, then cover and freeze while preparing the apples

Heat oven to 400°F/200°C. Peel and core the apples, then cut into wedges. Put the sugar and golden syrup in a flameproof 12cm ceramic tatin dish or non-stick pan and make sure it has a metal handle. Place over a medium-high heat.

Cook the golden syrup and sugar until it becomes a dark amber caramel syrup that's starting to smoke, then turn off the heat and stir in the 4oz diced chilled butter.

To assemble the tarte tatin, throw all the apples in the pan and add a little dusting of all the spices, about half a tsp each and caramelize for 5 minutes. Place the disc of frozen puff pastry on top – it will quickly defrost. Tuck the edges down the inside of the dish and baste with egg wash. With a knife, prick a few holes in the pastry to allow steam to escape. Bake for a further 30 mins until the pastry is golden brown and crisp.

Immediately turn out onto a plate and serve with crème fraîche or vanilla ice cream!

# NORWAY

## FINNMARK

We were in the Finnmark Alps on Norway's northernmost shores. Well inside the Arctic Circle but, thanks to the tail of the Gulf Stream, in mid-May the temperatures were bearable.

We were in kayaks barely wider than our bums, wearing an extra layer of Gore-Tex over our ski clothes: dry suits in case we capsized with excitement, with our skies tied to the aft. We were ski touring day and night as it never got dark but we did get a chance to enjoy some incredible proteins such as deer, whale, cod and salmon. Although I never caught any fish, nonetheless I did try. Even though it is classed as one of the easiest places to catch it in the world. Being a chef I feel like it's important to try and cook sustainably and locally and try to give back to the environment and not to over fish, so I wanted to share this incredible Salmon that I came across on my journey through Norway.

Kvarøy is a postcard-pretty Norwegian island and their mission is "to provide salmon of very high quality, without compromising either the environment or the welfare of the fish." The community and the company are redefining the salmon-farming industry through innovation and deep concern for the future of the fish we raise and the waters we live on. They have helped develop best-in-class farming techniques and a sustainable feed model. This has resulted in an omega-3 content that is twice as much as other farmed salmon. The flavor of Kvarøy Arctic salmon is informed by this breathtaking location. Fish have a merroir that reflects the waters in which they are raised. The Arctic waters are cold and clear, with a deep-fjord current that keeps the water fresh and helps exercise the salmon, reducing fat levels and giving this beautiful fish a pristine, clean flavor.

# TORCHED SALMON BRUSCHETTA

## WITH BEETROOT PUREE AND CURED ZUCCHINI

Serves 4

*The salmon is so wonderful and fresh here. It's almost a crime to cook it! I'm going to share a creative and fun way to enjoy it.*

## INGREDIENTS

Centre cut of the salmon

4 slices of Sourdough

3 zucchini's

½lb soft cream cheese

2 lemons, juiced

Arugula/ rocket

1 tin of cooked beetroot

2 tbsp red wine vinegar

Salt and black pepper

## METHOD

Grab a peeler and take the skin off the zucchini and put to waste, and then continue to peel the zucchini until you get to the seeds. Put the naked zucchini aside. Place the peeled zucchini in a bowl and dress with all the lemon juice, a pinch of salt and cracked black pepper then place in the fridge for 30 minutes.

Put your tin of beetroot including the juice in the blender, add a pinch of salt and a table spoon of red wine vinegar and purée. Place in the fridge.

Take the skin off the salmon and slice against the grain about 2cm wide and 0.5 cm thick, just like sashimi. You should end up with 6 slices per person, 24 in total. Place on a tray then sprinkle with sea salt and olive oil, cover with cling film and pop in the fridge.

Toast your sourdough under a grill, in a toaster, on a bbq -however you like, I prefer to spread butter on both sides of mine and caramelize in a pan on the stovetop. Remember color is flavor! Once you're happy with the coloring place on a board. Spread a thick layer of cream cheese on the sourdough then add cracked black pepper.

Grab the salmon out of the fridge and cover the sour dough with 6 slices each.

Now the fun part - blow torch the salmon just 10 seconds each piece. This provides a delicious charred flavor and allows all of the fat to be soaked up by the bread.

Get the zucchini and place it onto a kitchen towel to absorb the unwanted liquid.

Drizzle the beetroot puree over the salmon then place the cured zucchini on top.

The flavor and texture will blow your mind!

# CURED BEETROOT SALMON

## WITH HORSERADISH CREAM

Serves 6

## INGREDIENTS

**Horseradish cream**

½ lb Sour cream/ crème fraiche

2 tbsp of grated horseradish

1 tbsp of shredded fresh dill

CURED SALMON

1 trimmed side of salmon

5 raw beetroot, grated

1 tsp of fennel seeds

¼ of a cup, Gray Whale gin

1 tsp cardamom seeds

1 orange zested

1 tbsp of tarragon

1 cup of caster sugar

2 cups of sea salt

## METHOD

To make the salmon, peel the beetroot and cut into cubes. Blend the beetroot, fennel seeds, tarragon, cardamom, orange zest, Gray Whale gin, sugar and sea salt in a food processor to make the cure.

Pin bone and trim the salmon, lay it skin down into a rectangular dish and pour the cure over. Cover with cling film then leave in the fridge for 10 hours. Turn the salmon over and cure for another 20 hour.

Mix the horseradish, cream and dill together. Tip away the juices, wash off the cure and pat the salmon dry. At this stage your salmon is ready to slice and enjoy with that delicious horseradish cream on a bagel, a cracker, a waffle or even a salad!

# SALMON CAKES WITH MANGO

Serves 6

*Fiskeboller is the Norwegian term for fish balls, and is a dietary staple that can be discovered in practically every family home in this country. Hopefully they won't mind me adding a little Asian influence to it!*

## INGREDIENTS

**3 large potatoes , peeled**

**1lb of salmon, skin off and pin boned**

**1 lime zested and juiced**

**2 tbsp coriander shredded**

**1 tbsp of Thai green paste**

**1 soft mango**

**1 tbsp apple cider vinegar**

**Coconut oil for frying**

**Salt and pepper to taste**

## METHOD

First, boil the potatoes for around 40 minutes, let them cool, then peel and mash.

Puree your mango in a blender with a tbsp of apple cider vinegar.

Cut the salmon into 1 cm cubes and roast half at 400°F/200°C for 10mins then blitz the other half in a food processor with the Thai paste, lime juice, lime zest and shredded coriander.

Combine the cooked salmon and raw salmon with the mashed potatoes, then mold in the shape of your choosing. I like to use two spoons and make a quenelle but balls or croquettes work just fine.

Fry the salmon cakes in 5cm of coconut oil a few at a time depending on the size of the pan, or an air fryer will suffice until golden. Remove and transfer to a paper towel. Season to taste before serving with that sour mango puree and some fresh coriander leaves.

# NORWEGIAN WAFFLE

Serves 6

*The best thing about these waffles is that you can enjoy them either sweet or savory! Waffles in Norway are often thinner and softer than American or Belgian waffles. And they can be topped with anything from crème fraîche and caviar to strawberries and chattily cream or the highlight - cured salmon and a poached egg.*

## INGREDIENTS

6 large eggs

½ cup white sugar

1 tsp. ground cardamom

1 ½ cups all purpose flour

1 tsp. baking powder

½ tsp. salt

1 cup sour cream

½ cup butter (melted)

## METHOD

In a large bowl whip the eggs, sugar, and cardamom together until it is thick, pale yellow, and well aerated.

In a different bowl, combine the flour, baking powder, and salt. Set aside for later.

Mix the sour cream and butter into the egg and sugar mixture.

Combine the flour mixture and continue mixing until batter is thick and sticky.

Let the batter rest for 15-20 minutes at room temperature (this is important).

Preheat your waffle iron for 5 minutes.

Spray waffle iron with cooking spray and pour batter into the iron. Do not overfill or it will pour out the sides.

Cook until golden brown. Remove from waffle iron.

Top with whatever your heart desires!

# GRILLED SALMON

## WITH FENNEL, DILL AND PICKLED BEETROOT

Serves 4

### INGREDIENTS

**1lb salmon, pin boned and skinned**

**1 cup of picked dill**

**1 raw beetroot**

**1 fennel**

**Half a red onion**

**3 cups washed baby spinach leaves**

**3 tbsp of apple cider vinegar**

**1 lemon juiced**

**3 tbsps of roasted pumpkin seeds**

**1 tbsp of whole grain mustard**

**2 tbsp of olive oil**

**Sea salt**

### METHOD

Grab a mandolin and set it to a very thin setting. Then slice the fennel, red onion and beetroot and place into separate bowls.

Add a pinch of salt and the apple cider vinegar to the beetroot, wrap in cling film, and set aside. Mix the mustard into the lemon juice then dress the fennel with cling film and set aside.

Cut the salmon into 200g pieces and lightly brush with olive oil. Place it on a hot chargrill and sear for 30 seconds on both sides to get the lines and that charred flavor. Preheat the oven to 400°F/200°C and roast for 4 minutes, and then let it rest for 5 minutes.

This salad is great because it's so light and simple, and the acid really cuts through that fatty salmon!

# PAN-SEARED SALMON

METHOD

Get one side of salmon, skin it and pin bone it before slicing the tail off about 3 inches leading up, then 1 inch down from the head slice, then 2 inches in from the belly slice all the way along the length of the fish. I love to use these off cuts to make a Japanese salmon tartare.

Then slice into 4-6 depending on the size of the fish. My pieces are about 200g each.

I wanted to include this recipe because salmon is often overcooked. Before I cook salmon I like to remove it from the fridge and let it sit for 30 minutes coated with salt. This helps to give it a crispy skin as the salt will withdraw that moisture and it'll cook more evenly since the center will be closer to room temperature.

Score the skin evenly and neatly. This helps the filet lay more evenly along the bottom of the pan. The more you do, the crispier the salmon will be. My preference is 3 times.

Get your nonstick pan smoking hot then add 2 tbsp of coconut oil. Now add the salmon skin side down. You really want to keep it rendering for at least 3 minutes, then turn it down and do a final minute. Turn the heat back up and flip the salmon and sear for 2 minutes before turning onto the sides for 30 seconds each.

Set the oven to 400°F/200°C and place the salmon on top of some fresh thyme. This will stop it from overcooking from the bottom of the tray, and add flavor, of course! Bake no longer than 4 minutes. What you're looking for is for your salmon flesh to be rosy, not raw, but all most translucent. The temperature of the fish should hit 125°F.

Drain the excess juices from your beetroot and fennel and then mix in a large bowl with the dill, red onion, baby spinach, olive oil and pumpkin seeds. Now serve and enjoy the way the delicious acidity of this salad and its wonderful texture will really cut through that lovely fatty salmon. A perfect match!

# SALMON TARTARE

Serves 6

*This is incredible for canapés, a starter, or a main dish. Great quality salmon allows for such a simple dish to truly impress your guests!*

## INGREDIENTS

**8oz boneless salmon filet, skinless**

**1 tbsp finely diced, seeded**

**Cucumber**

**1 tbsp finely diced cornichons**

**1 tbsp finely diced shallot**

**1 tbsp small capers**

**1 tbsp finely diced chives**

FRENCH VINAIGRETTE

**2 tbsp. white wine vinegar**

**¼ tsp. fine sea salt (or to taste)**

**2 tsp. Dijon mustard**

**6 tbsp. extra virgin olive oil**

**1 lemon zested**

## METHOD

Place salmon on a plate and freeze until well chilled, about 20 minutes.

Add lemon zest, mustard and vinegar into a large bowl and whisk, while then adding the olive oil slowly until it emulsifies. Once the dressing is thick and smooth add the salt.

Thinly slice the salmon lengthwise into 1/8"-wide sheets. Cut each sheet into 1/8"-long strips. Cut strips crosswise into 1/8" cubes.

Add all the ingredients into the bowl. Season the tartare to taste with salt and pepper and then transfer the tartare to a bowl or a round ring.

If you want to make it more fun, I finished mine with a sous vide egg, some smoke.

# SW FRANCE

HOSSEGOR

I had the pleasure of opening two restaurants here with good friends until we were derailed by the covid shutdown. Known as the secret Riviera, here I found some of the best beach surf breaks in the world, coupled with wonderful pine forests that stretch for miles. Located close to Bordeaux, the wine is just one of many things worth indulging in here. Chanterelle mushrooms, Cepes, and some of the best poultry such as Magret de Canard and Poulet Fermier. A truly unique locale, it shares some of its heritage with Spain, and many traditional French dishes here incorporate the Espelette pepper for added spice. Boasting the most 3 star Michelin restaurants, San Sebastian, in my opinion, is the food hub of the planet. Whether dining at Murgaritz or Akellere, or enjoying the delicious tapas in the beautiful historic town, the cuisine found here is something truly special!

# DUCK BURGER WITH SMOKED CHEDDAR

## AND FIG CHUTNEY

Serves 6

## INGREDIENTS

**4 Magret duck breasts**

**1 cup grated smoked cheddar**

**1 tbsp smoked paprika**

**1 tbsp garlic powder**

**1 tbsp onion powder**

**2 tbsp chopped parsley**

**1 lemon zested**

**1 cup breadcrumbs**

FIG AND RED ONION CHUTNEY

**3 red onions sliced**

**½ a cup red wine vinegar**

**½ a cup red wine**

**½ cup granulated sugar**

**1 cinnamon stick**

**1 star anise**

**5 fresh figs in half (or fig jam)**

**1 tsp of orange zest**

**Salt and black pepper**

## METHOD

In my opinion, the key to making great chutney or marmalade is the caramel at the start. The intense heat of the sugar really produces unique tannin flavors from the dried spices.

Add sugar, cinnamon, star anise and orange zest to a heavy pot and place on a low heat until a caramel is formed.

Place olive oil in a pan on a medium heat and caramelize your onions and figs. Add salt and continue to sauté until it becomes a very light sandy color and figs are broken. Now add the figs, onions, red wine vinegar and red wine to the caramel and simmer until all the juice has reduced.

Finish with black pepper.

Cut your duck breast into 8 pieces and mince into a medium ground. You can ask your butcher to do it, or if you have a KitchenAid there's an attachment for mincing. There are cheap mincers online as well for about 50 dollars.

Add all the other ingredients and mix well, however, don't add salt as this will ruin the texture of the meat. You don't have to add breadcrumbs, but because the duck is so fatty it will make it easier to work with.

Mold into 6 equal balls and place in the fridge for 2 hours to set. Once set, take the balls and press down to create a flat surface area or place in a round ring, I like to keep the pates quite thick as I prefer to serve it rare, but this is optional.

In a hot pan, caramelize the pates for 2 minutes on each side. Season with salt on each as though cooking a steak, and baste using its own fat.

Preheat the oven to 400°F/200°C and place the pates on a tray, evenly adding the smoked hard cheese(I'm using sheep's cheese called Brebis) and bake for 8 minutes. Let rest for 5 minutes.

Grill the bun  - I love that charred flavor! Add some freshly washed spinach, the duck patty and a healthy spoonful of that sweet fig chutney.

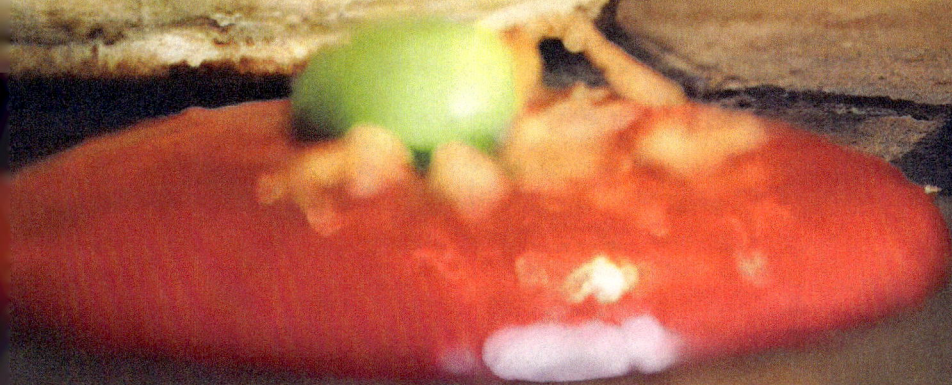

# BRIOCHE BUNS

Serves 6

## INGREDIENTS

4 large eggs

1 table spoon of instant yeast

3 ¾ cups all-purpose flour

2 ½ tablespoons sugar

1 teaspoon salt

12 tablespoons (1 ½ sticks)

Unsalted butter, room temperature

## METHOD

I would recommend using a kitchen aid, for this, using a paddle first Add the eggs into the mixing bowl, one at a time, Beat in 1 ¾ cups of the flour, the sugar, and salt. The dough will be sticky with a consistency of thick cake batter.

Switch to the dough hook and with the mixer on low speed, add the remaining 2 cups of flour in ½ cup increments.

When all of the flour has been incorporated, knead for 8 minutes on medium-low speed, stopping to scrape the down the dough hook occasionally. The dough will be firm but still sticky.

Let the dough rest for 10 minutes before incorporating the butter. (This allows the gluten to relax and makes incorporating the butter easier.)

With the mixer running on medium and the dough hook still attached, add the butter to the dough 1 tablespoon at a time. Wait until the butter has been fully incorporated before adding the next tablespoon.

After the final tablespoon has been added and incorporated into the dough, continue to knead for an additional 5 minutes.

Once the butter has been thoroughly absorbed, the dough will be soft and sticky. Scrape it into a clean bowl, shaping it loosely into a ball.

Cover the bowl with plastic wrap and let it rise at room temperature for 1 hour. Press the plastic wrap onto the surface of the dough and let rise in the refrigerator overnight (8 to 12 hours).
On a floured board, turn out the cold dough and press it into a flat circle that's about 1-inch thick. Cut the dough into 8 wedges. If you have a scale, weigh your dough (whole) and divide it by 8 to determine the weight of each bun so they will all be of equal size.
Hold a piece of dough in one hand and draw the edges in toward the center to form a ball. The dough will be quite soft and will not seem stretchy.

Place a dough ball on the board with the smooth side on top. Cup your fingers on one side of the roll and move it in a circular motion, drawing your cupped hand towards your thumb and using the friction on the board to shape it into a ball. Repeat with remaining rolls. You should not need to re-flour the board. You want a little stickiness to help you shape the balls

Line a baking sheet with parchment paper. Place the balls of dough 3 inches apart on the baking sheet and press them flat so they are about 3 ½ inches across. Cover the dough balls with a lightweight dish towel and let rise until puffy and almost doubled, about 1 ½ hours.

Towards the end of the rising time, preheat the oven to 400°F/200°C. Once doubled in size bake for 25 mins. Just remember color is flavor.

# CHARRED BASQUE OCTOPUS

## WITH GRILLED ZUCCHINI AND RED PEPPER

Serves 4

*The key to cooking octopus is to not damage the pink flesh or tentacles! That's what we render to make it crispy and get that charred flavor.*

## INGREDIENTS

1 large octopus

1 lemon, halved

1 celery bunch, roughly chopped

1 tsp fennel seeds

1 bunch of rosemary

1 onion, peeled and halved

2 cloves of peeled garlic

No Salt*

2 zucchinis

3 whole red bell peppers

1 cucumber

Tsp toasted sesame seeds

## METHOD

Get a large pot of water (the bigger the better) and add half a lemon, the celery, fennel seeds, bunch of rosemary, onion and garlic, and simmer for 5 minutes. This will infuse the water with flavor!

Now add the octopus and simmer for 90 minutes, being careful not to let the water boil as it will damage the flesh. Do not stir, just leave it be. The perfect temperature for the water is 180°F/90°C. You can also sous-vide if you have access to one.

Pre heat the oven to 400°F/200°C and chuck the peppers in for 45 minutes.

Remove from the oven and place them in ice water and peel away the outer skin. Chop in half, remove the seeds and stalk and then place in a blender, but don't blend yet.

Remove your octopus ideally with a spider as tongs will damage it and place on a cooling rack. Drain the stock into a colander. I do discard the stock as its quite salty but the vegetables are wonderful so add them to the peppers in the blender apart from the rosemary stalks. Now blitz to form a rustic puree. It can be blended until smooth but some extra texture is great with octopus.

Slice your zucchini at an angle about a cm thickness and place in a hot dry pan for about 2 minutes each side. We want to extract the water and get that charred flavor. Remember, color is flavor!

Now plate starting with the delicious red pepper sauce. I love garnishing octopus with cucumber because it really cleanses the pallet combined with the intense flavor of the meat. Sprinkle with toasted sesame seeds , and add a squeeze of lemon juice.

*Chef's Note*

*Fresh octopus is very salty, do not add any extra salt. You can use small amounts of the stock once it's cooked, but don't reduce it as it's inedible.

@_Schoph_

PLAGE DES
ESTAGNOTS

# DUCK CONFIT

Serves 6

*There isn't really any other dish that screams France more than duck confit. You will find it on every menu and it's delicious, tender and so easy to do.*

*Traditionally, in the South West of France it's used in a salade landaise, but I'm going teach you how to confit it. After that, the rest is up to you to imagine!*

## INGREDIENTS

**6 duck legs**

**2 tbsp rosemary**

**1 tsp pink peppercorns**

**2 tsp salt**

**3 cloves of peeled garlic**

**1l of duck fat but you can use sunflower oil**

## METHOD

Put the salt, garlic, peppercorns and rosemary in a blender and blitz, then rub the paste all over the duck legs. Put in the fridge for 24hrs but do not cover so the legs can dry out.

After 24hrs remove as much of the rub as you can with your hands, but don't wash. Then place in a half gastro and cover in oil, you can do it on the stove but you don't want to damage the skin or risk losing a bone - its very fragile.

Place parchment paper on top, this is called a cartouche. Then wrap with foil.

Pre heat the oven to 300°F/150°C and slowly roast for 6 hours.

Remove the ducks from the hot confit and then roast at 400°F/200°C for 20 minutes to really crisp that skin. Keep the fat and let it cool down before putting it in the fridge to use for more confit or banging roast potatoes.

That's it. This would cost at least 30 dollars in a restaurant, and instead now you have the main component and can go for the gold!

# SWEET FRENCH TOAST

Serves 4

*Pastis landais is a traditional French pastry. It's made with a combination of eggs, butter, flour, yeast, and powdered sugar. The pastry is typically flavored with vanilla, rum, and orange blossom water. Once baked, pastis landais is golden yellow in color and its exterior is crunchy because it's sprinkled with large pieces of sugar on top.*

*I wanted to create this classic with a twist, using stale brioche buns and more accessible ingredients. Here I merged two French classics - pastis landais and pain perdu (French Toast). My take is on the sweet side.*

## INGREDIENTS

**4 Stale brioche burger buns**

**1 orange zested**

**2 eggs**

**1 cup of milk**

**4 tbsp honey**

**4 cinnamon sticks**

**4 tsp vanilla essence**

**4 tbsp amaretto**

**4oz of hard butter, cut into 4**

**4 tsp brown sugar**

FOR GARNISH

**Fresh berries**

**Plain yoghurt**

**Toasted walnuts**

## METHOD

Mix the eggs, milk, vanilla and orange zest together to make a custard.

Top and tale  your buns to make them flat either side then dip them in the custard.

Put a hot non stick pan on the heat and then pop the brioche in. You can do two at a time, leaving for 30 seconds before flipping. Cut the butter into 4 chunks and add one in with 1 cinnamon stick, 1 tbsp of honey, 1 tsp brown sugar and a tbsp of amaretto. Caramelize for 1 minute, continually basting, then turn and baste again until golden dark brown. Repeat the process.

Serve this delicious French toast with fresh berries and yoghurt with toasted walnuts.

Mushrooms are in season September through to October but you can find them all summer with the right weather conditions!

Ceps mushrooms have a stocky, balanced shape and an earthy, undergrowth-like smell. Their shape makes them easy to spot, especially on patches of moss where they often grow.

In terms of flavor, they are popular with top chefs and the general public in France. They have firm flesh and a strong smell.

Chanterelle mushrooms are called girolles in France, and they can be used in so many different ways. Put them in pastas; they work well with creamy sauces. Or roast them and include them in salads. They may also be enjoyed for breakfast, combined with arugula and fresh herbs for a hearty omelet.

The next Paragraph is to share how to cook mushrooms correctly! They are delicate but the key is to get rid of the water first in order to caramelize. I'm a fungi but there ain't muchshroom for a soggy mushroom!

The best way to prepare mushrooms is to get a pastry brush and dust the mud off. You want to try to avoid getting them wet.

Roast them in the oven at 400°F for 30 minutes, as this will pull the water out. Take them out and pop them on a kitchen towel. Now you're ready to sauté.

Chuck on a medium sized pan, with a tbsp. of olive oil and a tbsp of butter, then add the mushrooms and watch them become golden brown and crisp up nicely. This gives them an amazing texture, trust me! You can add a garlic paste and some cream for a pasta sauce, or even just to dip a fresh baguette into it. Or lay off the cream and deglaze the pan with a balsamic caramel a make a lush mushroom marmalade. Have it on toast and call it a mushroom on croute.

# UKRAINE

LVIV

The war in Ukraine began shortly after I'd completed filming for Below Deck Mediterranean. Having been immersed in the yachting industry for years, I felt weighed down by the constant exposure to the superficial aspects of life. I had such a strong desire to find a way to give back, so I flew to Poland and made my way to the Ukraine border. For the next six weeks I dedicated myself fully to cooking with World Central Kitchen. Some of the most powerful memories, bonds and friendships I'll ever have were created during my experience there. José Andréa and his incredible team made it their mission to bring hope to so many people who had lost everything. The impact it had on me is something I'll carry with me forever.

Many people in this world seek no recognition and they just keep giving. Karla Hoyos, Noah Simms and Eric Gephart, thank you x

# UKRAINE BORSCHT

## WITH DILL AND SOUR CREAM

Serves 6                                          Inspired by Noah Mountain Man Simms

## INGREDIENTS

3 medium beets, peeled, grated

4 tbsp olive oil divided

2l veg stock

3 medium Yukon potatoes, peeled
and sliced into bite-sized pieces

2 carrots, peeled and grated


MIREPOIX

Celery, trimmed, finely chopped

1 red bell pepper, finely chopped,
optional

1 onion, finely chopped

1 can white cannellini beans with
their juice

2 bay leaves

2-3 tbsp red wine vinegar or to
taste

1 tsp salt or to taste

¼ tsp cracked black pepper

1 large garlic clove, diced

3 tbsp chopped dill

1 tbsp paprika

## METHOD

Peel, grate and/or slice all vegetables (keeping sliced potatoes in cold water
to prevent browning until ready to use then drain).

Heat a large soup pot over medium/high heat and add 2 tbsp olive oil. Add
grated beets and sauté for 10 minutes, stirring occasionally until beets are
softened.

Add 2 liters of stock. Add sliced potatoes and grated carrots then cook for
10-15 minutes.

While potatoes are cooking, place a large skillet over medium/high heat and
add 2 Tbsp oil. Add chopped onion, celery and bell pepper. Sauté, stirring
occasionally until softened and lightly golden (7-8 minutes). Add paprika and
stir fry for 30 seconds then transfer to the soup pot to continue cooking with
the potatoes.

When potatoes and carrots reach desired softness, add 1 can of beans with
their juice, 2 bay leaves, 2-3 tbsp red wine vinegar, 1 tsp salt, ¼ tsp black
pepper, and 1 diced garlic clove. Simmer for an additional 2-3 minutes and
add more salt and vinegar to taste. Finish with 3 tbsp chopped dill and a
dollop of sour cream.

# CHICKEN KIEV

## WITH BURRATA AND CHIVE

---

Serves 4

## INGREDIENTS

---

**4 chicken breasts (with or without the wing bone)**

**½ lb butter (soft)**

**4 cloves garlic , chopped**

**½ lb cream cheese**

**1 medium sized burrata**

**3 tbsp finely chopped chives**

**4 tbsp very finely chopped parsley**

**4 eggs, beaten**

**2 cups of flour**

**3 cups of breadcrumbs**

**Salt**

**Pepper**

**Chili powder**

**Vegetable oil (for frying)**

## METHOD

---

In a bowl, add the butter, tarragon, parsley, ricotta and garlic. Season with salt, pepper and add a pinch of chili powder. Mix well.

Rip off a peace of grease proof paper and place the butter mix 2 cm from the end and then roll it in the shape of a cylinder about 4 to 5 inches long. Place this cylinder in the freezer for 1 hour.

Thoroughly clean the chicken from its tendons. Four breasts will produce 4 large and 4 small separate pieces.

Extract the chicken breast filets lengthwise.

Between two sheets of plastic wrap, beat the 8 pieces of chicken using the smooth side of the mallet and flatten them into ¼ inch thickness. Season with salt and pepper.

Take the butter out of the freezer and cut it into 4 pieces of equal length.

Place the butter in the centre of each pounded small piece of breast filet, and wrap it well, giving it a long shape.

Lay the four larger pieces of filets flat and place each piece stuffed with butter in the centre of each filet. Wrap tightly and give an elliptical shape. The surface should be very smooth.

Place them in the freezer for 30 minutes.

Heat a large quantity of oil in a deep pan and bring it to 340°F/160°C.

Meanwhile, remove the fillets from the freezer and roll each of them in the flour first, then in the beaten egg and finally in the breadcrumbs.

Roll each fillet a second time in the egg and then in the breadcrumbs.

Dip the breaded stuffed filets in hot oil and fry them on both sides for a few minutes until they get a nice crust and a golden color.

Place in a baking dish.

During frying, preheat the convection oven to 400°F/200°C.

Bake the fried filets for 15 to 20 minutes, depending on the thickness.

Traditionally this is served with a creamy mashed potato, and if there's any leftover filling it can be heated up and served as extra sauce.

# DRANIKI OR DERUNY

## (POTATO CAKES)

Serves 8

*The great thing about this cake is that you can serve anything with it or ideally on it, like pulled pork or brisket and even a poached egg with hollandaise. Its sometimes nice to keep it vegetarian and serve a delicious beetroot salad on the side.*

### INGREDIENTS

6 medium potatoes

1 egg

3 heaped tablespoons of flour

1 medium white onion

1 tsp salt

½ tsp pepper

4 tbsp sunflower oil

2-3 cloves of garlic, optional

Dill and Parsley – handful, optional

### METHOD

Grate the potatoes and add them to a bowl. In the bowl, add 1 tsp of salt, mixing it in. Leave the mixture for around 5-7 minutes.

Squeeze the liquid out of the potatoes with your hands or using a cheesecloth, depending on preference.

Now with the potato prepared, grate the onion and add it to the drained potatoes.

Crack open the egg into a separate bowl, beat the egg, and finally add it to the potato-onion mixture.

Next, add the black pepper and any additional ingredients you're using, such as minced garlic, dill, and parsley.

Add the flour to the mixture, and mix everything together thoroughly. Once mixed, it should be a batter similar to pancake batter.

On a pan over medium-high heat, add 1 tbsp of oil. When the oil is simmering, turn the heat down to medium, and add a scoop of batter at a time, forming little potato pancakes. Cook for about 3 minutes on one side until it's brown on the bottom.

After about 3 minutes, once the draniki are brown on the bottom, flip them to cook on the other side. Turn the heat down to medium-low and cover the pan with a lid, if possible, so that the potato will cook better on the inside. You'll be cooking them for another 3-4 minutes until the potato is cooked inside.

# BEET SALAD

Serves 6

## INGREDIENTS

**2 cups beetroot, cooked, chopped**

**3 tbsp of chopped dill**

**2 cucumbers, peeled, seeded, diced**

**1 red onion, peeled, finely sliced**

**2 carrots, peeled, thinly sliced**

**2 tbsp of plain yoghurt**

**Seasoning**

## METHOD

Mix all the ingredients together and pop it on top of the potato pancakes and your good to go.

# UKRAINIAN POTATO SALAD

## WITH BRAISED LAMB SHANK

Serves 4

*The key to cooking octopus is to not damage the pink flesh or tentacles! That's what we render to make it crispy and get that charred flavor.*

### INGREDIENTS

**4 lamb shanks**

**2 tins chopped tomatoes**

**3 cloves of garlic**

**1 onion**

**2 carrots, peeled, rough chop**

**1 bunch Rosemary**

**2 cups chicken stock**

**1 onion, rough chop**

POTATO SALAD

**2 large Yukon potatoes, peeled**

**2 large carrots, peeled**

**7 eggs**

**8-9 kosher pickles , diced**

**500g of bacon lardons**

**1 large red onion**

**1 (15oz) canned sweet peas**

**Mayonnaise for dressing**

**1 tbsp chopped parsley**

**1 tbsp of chopped dill**

**1 lemon juiced**

**1 tsp whole grain mustard**

### LAMB SHANK METHOD

First pre heat the oven to 400°F/200°C and place the shanks in the oven for 20 minutes to brown them off, ideally in a deep tray. This will render the fat, add to flavor and keep in all those juices.

Then add all the remaining ingredients to the browned shanks . Make sure the lamb is covered by the tomato stock and mirepoix. Add salt and place in parchment paper then close with foil to prevent them drying out. Place in a pre heated oven at 300°F/150°C and braise for 4 hours. You could put this in the oven and walk away, go enjoy the day without having to worry!

### POTATO SALAD METHOD

Dice the raw carrots and potatoes and then add to boiling salted water for about 12 minutes. Rinse with cold water and drain well on paper towels. In a separate pot, put the eggs in salted cold water. Bring to a boil for 8 minutes total. Cool them down in cold water, peel then chop.

Crisp the lardons in a hot pan rendering all the fat until nice and crispy.

Dice the pickles and red onion, then add all the ingredients together except the peas as we don't want to crush them. Mix with the mayonnaise, lemon juice and whole grain mustard. Finally, fold the peas in along with the chopped parsley.

Now, take the lamb out and gently remove the shanks from the tray. They should be falling off the bone. Skim the fat off the top of the stock and discard.

The remaining stock can be blended until smooth. Now all that's left is to plate and enjoy!

# HOLUBTSI

Serves 6

*Holubtsi are traditional Ukrainian cabbage rolls, especially popular in the Carpathians region. While holubtsi are usually stuffed with minced meat, the dish can be made vegetarian with plain rice or buckwheat. Cabbage is boiled to soften the leaves, which are then filled with minced pork or beef, browned onions and carrots, mushrooms, and cooked rice.*

## INGREDIENTS

1 white cabbage

1lb ground pork

1 cup white rice

2 tbsp sunflower oil

1 yellow onion: some for the filling and some for the sauce

2 cloves of garlic

2 peeled carrots

2 tins chopped tomatoes

1 tbsp tomato paste

2 Bay leaves

Celery salt

Freshly ground black pepper

Sour cream

Fresh dill

## METHOD

Cook the rice in a small saucepan for 5 minutes, then strain and set aside.

Bring a large pot of salted water to a boil. Cut the core out of the bottom of the cabbage and carefully remove about 12 leaves. (We're cooking a few extra just in case we need them.) I usually just peel back the top of the leaf a little, then lift from the bottom gently until it releases. It's okay if it tears a bit here and there.

Blanch 2 cabbage leaves at a time for about 2-3 minutes, until they are softened but still bright green. Set aside to cool.

Dice the onion finely and divide in two. Grate the carrot on a box grater.

Add 1 tablespoon of the sunflower oil to a large, deep skillet with a lid over medium heat. Add half the diced onions and cook until just beginning to caramelize and brown, 5-8 minutes. Remove from the pan and set aside.

Add the remaining sunflower oil back into the same pan and reduce heat to medium low.

Add the grated carrot and remaining diced onion along with a pinch of kosher salt and cook, stirring frequently until the vegetables are soft, but not taking on any color.

Add the tomato paste and cook, stirring constantly, for one minute.
Add the crushed tomatoes, reserved water in the can, the bay leaf, and ½ teaspoon of salt. Bring to a low simmer for about 5 minutes and then turn heat off.

Combine the ground pork, rice, the reserved cooked onions, 1 ½ teaspoons of salt and ½ teaspoon of pepper in a large bowl. Use your hands to gently mix all ingredients together until the rice, meat and onions are evenly distributed throughout.

Divide the filling into 8 equal parts. Lay the cabbage leaf so it is curved side up with the thicker stem end toward you. Place 1/8 of the filing at the bottom of the cabbage leaf and gently roll away from you.

Fold each side of the leaf toward the center. Continue to roll away from you until the meat filling is entirely encased in the cabbage leaf.

Place in the pan of sauce seam-side down.

Continue with remaining cabbage and filling.

Cover the pan and cook over low heat for 40-50 minutes until the pork is cooked through. Serve immediately.

# CANDIED PRUNES STUFFED WITH WALNUTS

## AND FINISHED WITH CREAM

Serves 6

### INGREDIENTS

**17.5oz of pitted prunes**

**3.5oz of walnuts**

**⅔ cup of water**

**2 tbsp brown sugar**

**1 cup double or heavy cream**

**1 tbsp powdered sugar**

**1 tsp vanilla extract**

**Chocolate to grate on top of the**

**cream when serving**

### METHOD

First add the water and the sugar to a pot. Place the pot over medium-low heat on the stove and stir for a couple of minutes while the sugar dissolves.

Then, stuff the prunes with walnuts and place them in the same pot.

Place a lid over the pot and put the pot on the stove over low heat and reduce, we want to candied the prunes for about 10-15 minutes. Then lift the lid and make sure the liquid has evaporated and the liquid is now syrup. If not, keep simmering the prunes until you have a caramel. Once done, remove the pot from the heat and let the prunes cool

Add 1 tbsp of powdered sugar (icing sugar) and a tsp of vanilla extract to 300 ml of double cream. Grab a hand mixer, pour the cream in a large bowl and whip the cream with the hand mixer until you get soft peaks.

I like to serve the prunes in a glass and layer them with cream in multiple layers, topping them with some grated chocolate. Absolutely banging!

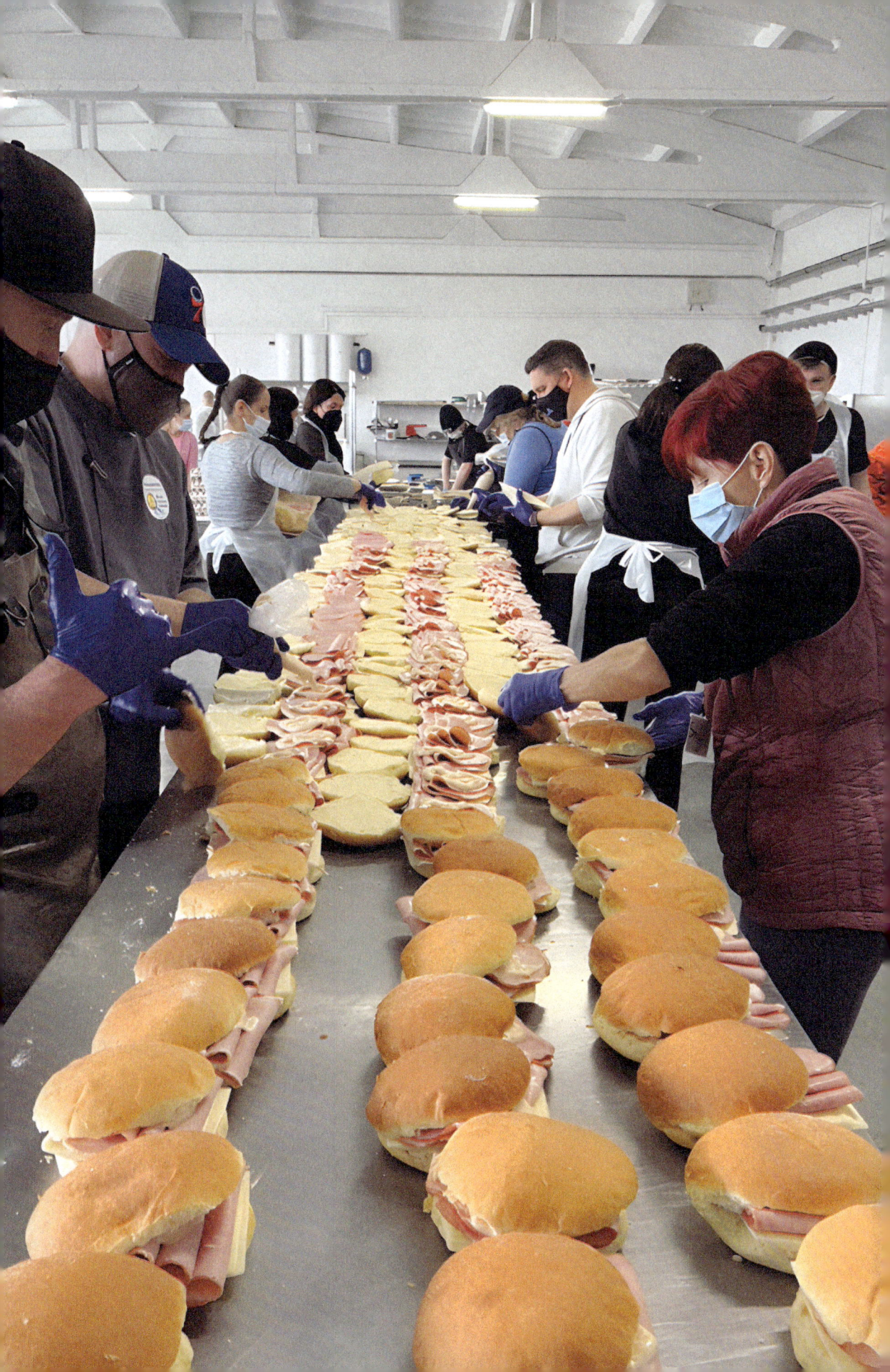

# NEPAL AND TIBET

## MOUNT EVEREST

My expedition climbing the North Side of Mount Everest was the experience of a lifetime, and I'm who I am today due to having done it. I've always believed in the importance of pushing myself physically to change my mental state, and this trip would test every limit I had. Beyond the immense power of that mountain was the power and hospitality of the people who call Nepal and Tibet home. Sherpas whose supernatural ability to safely guide those as crazy as me on the mountain, and the locals with open arms who welcomed me like family. The journey took me through India, Nepal and Tibet so I'm honored to share a few dishes in these pages from destinations whose incredible food deserves as much recognition as the mountain itself.

Training at advanced Base Camp 6400 meters.

NEPAL

# RED LENTIL DAHL SOUP

## WITH A POACHED EGG

Serves 6

### INGREDIENTS

**1 cup red lentils**

**1l vegetable broth**

**1 tbsp coconut oil**

**1 tsp cumin seeds**

**1 tsp black mustard seeds**

**1 onion finely diced**

**A knob of ginger grated**

**2 tsp ground coriander**

**2 tsp ground turmeric**

**½ tsp cayenne pepper**

**1 small tin of chopped tomato**

**1 tin of light coconut milk**

**Salt goes a long way in this dish**

### METHOD

Wash the red lentils, drain and set aside.

Add the lentils to a medium-sized saucepan and cover with the vegetable broth.

Bring to a boil and then turn down the heat, cover and cook 20 to 23 minutes.

While the lentils are cooking, in a skillet heat the oil to medium-high.

Add the cumin seeds and mustard seeds. Within a few seconds, they will begin to pop.

Add the chili and onions and sauté over medium heat for about 10 minutes until the onions are translucent.

Add the fresh ginger, ground coriander, turmeric, and cayenne pepper. Cook just to heat through, about 30 seconds.

Now add the chopped tomatoes and cook for about 5 minutes before removing from the heat. Add the lentils and stock to the sauté and deglaze, and then add the salt and coconut milk and heat through.

Add your egg to vinegar water and poach till soft, place on top and finish with coriander.

# CHICKEN THUKPA

Serves 4

*Thukpa is a Himalayan noodle soup, usually served with meat, and is especially delicious with lean chicken. It is popular in Tibet, Bhutan, Nepal, and some parts of India. "Thuk" means heart so it is a heart-warming dish. In Bhutan it would usually be made with buckwheat noodles.*

## INGREDIENTS

2 carrots sliced

1 red pepper sliced

1 celery stick, julienned

½ lb baby spinach, fresh

4 chicken thighs, deboned

2 cups chicken broth

1lb rice noodles

1 clove garlic minced

1 knob ginger, minced

1 red-hot chili pepper sliced

1 punit cherry tomatoes

2 shallots, peeled

1 tbsp cilantro, shredded

½ tsp ground cumin

½ tsp Szechwan pepper

½ tsp ground turmeric

1 lime juiced

1 tbsp coconut oil

Salt to taste

## METHOD

Start by pan-frying the chicken thigh until there's a nice color and it's seared, no need to cook all the way, and then set aside.

Soak the dry rice noodles in warm water for an hour then drain.

Make soup paste by combining garlic, ginger, hot chili pepper, cherry tomatoes, shallots, cilantro, ground cumin, and ground turmeric, Szechwan pepper and lime juice are then added into the blender or food processor and blended until smooth.

Add soup paste to the same chicken pan and fry for 30 seconds or so. Pour in chicken broth and mix well. Bring to a boil and reduce heat to low.

Add prepared vegetables and chicken and simmer 15 minutes or until carrots are tender and chicken is cooked

Add the noodles and season with salt, then simmer for 2 minutes until the noodles are al dente. To serve, divide rice noodles between bowls, pour soup over and garnish with fresh cilantro.

# BUTTER CHICKEN WITH EASY NAAN BREAD

Serves 4

*I do like to cook my naan on a chargrill but I understand that isn't possible for most so in this recipe you can use a skillet.*

## INGREDIENTS

2 cups plain yoghurt, full fat

1 tbsp lemon juice

1 tsp tumeric powder

2 tsp garam masala

½ tsp chili powder

1 tsp ground cumin

1 tbsp ginger, freshly grated

2 cloves garlic, crushed

½ lb chicken thigh fillets, cut into bite-size pieces

## INGREDIENTS FOR CURRY SAUCE

2 tbsp of butter

1 tbsp coconut oil

1 tbsp tomato puree

1 cup double cream

1 tbsp coconut sugar

1 ¼ tsp salt

## MARINADE METHOD

Marinade: Combine the marinade ingredients with the chicken in a bowl.

Cover and refrigerate overnight, or up to 24 hours (minimum 3 hours).

To cook the chicken, heat the coconut oil in a large fry pan. Take the chicken out of the marinade but do not wipe or shake off the marinade from the chicken. Also be sure not to pour the marinade left in the bowl into the frying pan.

Place chicken in the frying pan and cook for around 3 minutes, or until the chicken is white all over (it doesn't really brown because of the marinade).

For the sauce, add the tomato paste, cream, sugar, butter and salt. Turn down to low and simmer for 20 minutes. Do a taste test to see if it needs more salt.

Garnish with coriander or cilantro leaves if using. Serve with basmati rice and easy naan bread.

NAAN METHOD (Next Page)

## INGREDIENTS

### EASY GARLIC NAAN BREAD

**1 tsp instant / rapid rise yeast**

**½ cup warm tap water**

**1 tbsp white sugar**

**2 tbsp yoghurt**

**1 ½ tbsp whisked egg**

**½ tsp salt**

**2 cups all-purpose/plain**

**2 tbsp unsalted butter, melted**

### FINISHES

**30g / 2 tbsp butter, melted**

**1 small garlic clove**

**Nigella seeds**

**Coriander, finely chopped**

## NAAN METHOD

Mix yeast with warm water and sugar in a small bowl. Cover with cling wrap, leave for 10 minutes until foamy.

Egg and yoghurt: Whisk together.

Flour: Sift flour and salt into a separate bowl.

Add wet ingredients: Make a well in the flour, add yeast mixture, and butter and egg mixture. Mix together with a spatula. Once the flour is mostly incorporated, switch to your hands and bring it together into a ball. No kneading is required.

Proof 1: Cover the bowl with cling-wrap, then leave in a warm place for 1 – 1.5 hrs until it doubles in size.

Cut into 6 pieces: Place the dough on a lightly floured surface. Cut into 6 equal pieces, then shape into balls with a smooth surface by stretching the surface and tucking it under

Proof 2: Place balls on a lightly-floured tray or plate. Sprinkle lightly with flour, cover loosely with a lightweight damp tea towel. Put in a warm place to rise for 15 minutes until it increases in size by about 50%.

Roll out: Place a round on a lightly-floured work surface, flatten with your hand. Roll out into 3 – 4mm / 0.12 – 0.16" thick rounds (about 16cm / 6.5" wide).

I like to do on and open flame BBQ but its easier to do in a skillet.

Heat skillet: Rub a cast iron skillet with a very light coat of oil using ½ tsp oil on a paper towel. Set over high heat until you see wisps of smoke

Cook naan: Place a naan dough in the skillet and cook for 1 to 1 ½ minutes until the underside is deep golden / slightly charred – the surface should get bubbly. Flip then cook the other side for 1 minute until the bubbles become deep charred brown.

Cook remaining naan: Remove, set aside, and repeat with remaining naan, taking care to regulate the heat of the skillet so it doesn't get too hot.

Finishing: Melt butter and simmer crushed garlic for 3 mins on a low heat then brush freshly cooked naan with garlic butter and sprinkle with nigella seeds and coriander.

Serve hot!

# ONION BHAJIS WITH RAITA

Serves 6

## INGREDIENTS

**3 red onions, finely sliced**

**2 lemons juiced**

**100g chick pea flour**

**½ tsp gluten-free baking powder**

**½ tsp chili powder**

**½ tsp turmeric**

**1 green chili, deseeded and very finely chopped**

**1 tsp salt**

**Vegetable oil for frying**

### FOR THE RAITA

**½ cucumber**

**1 cup Greek-style yogurt**

**2 tbsp chopped mint**

## METHOD

Soak the onion in the lemon juice and salt, sift the flour and baking powder into a bowl, and then add the chilli powder, turmeric, and chopped chili.

For the raita, peel the cucumber and grate it into a sieve set over another bowl. Mix the remaining ingredients with some seasoning and the drained cucumber – squeezing out any extra moisture with your hands. Now spoon into a small serving bowl.

Add the dry mix to the onions and mix well. Heat about 5cm of oil in a wok or deep pan, but do not fill the pan more than a third full. Add a tiny speck of batter. If it rises to the surface surrounded by bubbles and starts to brown, then the oil is hot enough for frying.

Lower heaped tbsps of the bhaji mixture into the pan, a few at a time. Cook for a few minutes, turning once, until they are evenly browned and crisp, so about 3-4 minutes. Drain on a paper towel, sprinkle with a little salt and keep warm while you cook the rest. Serve with the raita.

# JAPAN

NISEKO

This was a land of pure magic. To be able to enjoy pristine powdery snow followed by a traditional Onsen, their natural hot springs, is heaven on Earth. Not to mention a delicious Sapporo!

In this photo is Mount Yotei, also known as Mt Fuji of Hokkaido. If you're lucky enough to get a clear weather day you can ride the crater of the volcano!

# ROASTED PORK BELLY

## WITH A MISO, SHITAKE MUSHROOM AND COCONUT SAUCE

Serves 6

### INGREDIENTS

1lb skin off and boned pork belly

2 tins of light coconut milk

8 sliced shitake mushrooms

MISO BASE

1 tbsp of white miso paste

1 tsp tomato paste

2 cloves of peeled garlic

1 onion diced

1 lemon grass shredded

1 tsp chili paste

1 tbsp. coconut oil

1 tsp fish sauce

1 tbsp coconut sugar

Garnishes - shredded coriander
and spring onions

### METHOD

Pre heat the oven to 400°F/200°C and salt the pork belly, then bake for 45 minutes. No extra oil is needed because of the high fat content.

For the miso base, blitz all the ingredients in a blender. Put a pot on a medium heat then add the oil and sauté the base. After 1 minute add the mushrooms and caramelize.

Once there's a golden color on the mushrooms add the coconut milk, sugar and fish sauce and then reduce by half.

Remove the pork belly and let it rest for 10 minutes. Now cut into four pieces and caramelize in a hot pan for 2 minutes each side, removing the excess fat as you go.

Serve with white rice and garnish with coriander and spring onions.

# JAPANESE BEEF AND BEETROOT TARTARE

Serves 6

## INGREDIENTS

½ lb of fresh beef fillet finely diced

2 shallots finely diced

1 cup of  cooked beetroot grated

1 tbsp of grated ginger

1 tbsp of sesame oil

2 tbsp mushroom soy

2 tbsp sweet chili sauce

1 tbsp shredded coriander

4 egg yolks

½ a cup of rice wine vinegar

½ a cup of soy

GARNISH

Root vegetable chips (shop
bought)

## METHOD

Separate 4 eggs and discard the whites or set aside and use for meringue.

Place the yolks gently in a bowl, add a pinch of salt, the rice wine vinegar and soy sauce. Put in the fridge for 3 hours, which will lightly cure the yolks.

Combine all the other ingredients together apart from the nuts and mix into a bowl.

Serve in a bowl or use a round ring for presentation, place the cured yolk on top, and then finish with the root vegetable chips.

# HAMACHI NIGIRI (YELLOWTAIL)

Serves 10

*The hardest thing about this dish is probably getting the fish but you can do it with anything you can get your hands on, like sushi grade tuna or salmon.*

## INGREDIENTS

**2 cups Japanese short-grain white rice**

**⅓ cup rice vinegar, plus more for shaping**

**3 tablespoons sugar**

**1 ½ teaspoon kosher or sea salt**

**20 slices sushi-grade raw fish**

**Soy sauce and wasabi to serve**

## METHOD

When cooking the rice I like to use a rice cooker, it's a controlled temperature and means you can just walk away.

The type of rice you use matters. I prefer Nishiki, which is easy to find and regarded as high-quality, good sushi rice. My Japanese friends say it's the best!

Make the sushi rice. In a large bowl, use your fingers to wash the rice with cold water until the water is almost clear, changing the water frequently (about 2-4 times). Soak the clean rice in fresh cold water for 30 minutes. Drain the rice in a fine-mesh sieve.

Cook the rice on the stovetop or in an electric rice cooker. If cooking on the stovetop, combine the rice and 2 cups of water in a medium pot over medium heat. Cover and bring to a boil, then reduce the heat to low and cook until the water is completely absorbed—about 12 minutes. If using a rice cooker, use the "sushi" setting if available and the amount of water indicated for three cups of rice.

In a small saucepan, combine the vinegar, sugar, and salt over medium-high heat. Bring to a boil and whisk until the sugar dissolves.

Wet the inside of a large bowl with a damp cloth and transfer the cooked rice to the slightly wet bowl, leaving behind any rice that's stuck to the bottom of the pot. Pour the hot vinegar mixture over the rice. Use a spatula to slice through the rice at a 45-degree angle, flipping the rice over in between strokes.

Once the rice is completely mixed, cover the bowl with a clean, damp kitchen towel until ready to use. You want warm rice when making sushi.

Prepare a small bowl of ice water with a splash of rice vinegar.

Dip your hands into the water and use your damp hands to grab a small ball of sushi rice.

Using your hands, form the rice into a rectangle about as long as one slice of fish.

Top the rice ball with a slice of fish and gently squeeze the rice and fish together in one hand, don't over squeeze as it will make the rice to chewy.

Repeat steps.

# PORK RAMEN

Serves 6

*You can make this delicious soup with any meat you desire. I just love pork belly because it's packed full of flavor and so easy to do.*

## INGREDIENTS

**1lb ramen noodles**

**Drizzle sesame oil**

**6 cups toridashi stock**

**1oz fresh root ginger, 4 thin slices**

**2 garlic cloves, slice thinly**

**8 fresh shiitake mushrooms, cut thin**

**1 carrot, cut into matchsticks**

**7oz bean sprouts**

**1¾oz sliced bamboo shoots**

**3½oz enoki mushrooms**

**1lb/2oz pork belly, skinned, boned**

**2 spring onions, cut diagonally**

**1 long red chili, finely sliced**

**4 soft boiled eggs and then halved**

**1 tbsp shredded coriander**

## METHOD

Pre heat the oven to 400°F/200°C, salt the pork belly and then bake for 45 minutes. No extra oil is needed because of the high fat content.

Once the pork is ready let it cool and slice as thin as you can. This is also great to do if you have any left over pork as its so easy to work with.

Cook the noodles following the instructions on the packet. Once cooked, drain and drizzle with a little sesame oil to stop the noodles from sticking.

Heat the stock in a large pan with the ginger, garlic, shiitake mushrooms and carrots.

Simmer for 5-8 minutes.

Carefully arrange the warm noodles, beansprouts, bamboo shoots, enoki mushrooms, choi sum and sliced pork in four large serving bowls.

Pour the stock over the pork and vegetables with a ladle. Top with the spring onions and sliced chili.

Half the eggs and place on the top of each serving.

# CHICKEN TERIYAKI

Serves 4

## INGREDIENTS

2 tbsp toasted sesame oil

4 skinless and boneless chicken thighs

2 large garlic cloves, crushed

1 thumb-sized piece of ginger, grated

1 tbsp honey

½ cup light soy sauce

1 tbsp rice wine vinegar

1 tbsp sesame seeds, to garnish

4 spring onions, shredded

Noodles or rice of choice, to serve

Charred bok choi, to serve

## METHOD

Heat the oil in a non-stick pan over a medium heat. Add the chicken and fry for 7 minutes, or until golden. Add the garlic and ginger and fry for 2 minutes. Stir in the honey, soy sauce, and vinegar and a splash of water.

Bring to a boil and cook for 2 - 5 minutes over a medium heat while continuing to baste until the chicken is sticky and coated in a thick sauce.

Remove the chicken and toss in the bok choi and sauté for 2 minutes.

Scatter over the spring onions and sesame seeds, then serve the chicken with the noodles or rice and charred bok choi. You can just serve with a side of soy sauce as well, which is very light and delicious!

# HIBACHI SHRIMP WITH YUZU UDON NOODLES

Serves 4

## INGREDIENTS

**1 tbsp of coconut oil**

**1 lb of peeled large shrimp**

**3 tbsp of soy sauce**

**2 cloves of garlic, finely minced**

**1 tbsp of sesame oil**

**1 tbsp of yuzu or 1 lemon, juiced**

**Half a white onion sliced**

**1 handful of baby corn halved**

**1 handful of sliced zucchini**

**1 handful of snow peas**

## METHOD

Soak the udon noodles in warm water for 1 hour.

I like to fire up my charcoal grill for this to get that smokey flavor through the prawns but it can be done this way as well. Heat the coconut oil in a large skillet over medium heat then add the shrimp and cook for about 2 minutes, either side, then remove and rest.

Add in the soy sauce, garlic, sesame oil, zuchinni , onions, sautéed for 1 minute.

Drain the noodles, add them to the pan with the yuzu, snow peas and the baby corn then place a lid on top. Steam for 5 minutes. We want there to be a little bite to these noodles. Then serve, simple and delicious.

# UNITED STATES

FLORIDA

After tearing both ACLs in a bad skiing accident, I was struggling deeply with depression and suicidal thoughts. I was suffering both mentally and physically, but rather than give in to the pain I changed my surroundings instead. I began working on a new yacht in West Palm Beach, Florida. Feeling lost and knowing no one, it was a tough start. In time though I met an incredible group of people who took me in and who I now consider to be some of my closest friends. Florida started to feel like home, and a second chance. I also found an outlet for my adrenaline craving in the form of skydiving. Since then I've continued to enjoy this thrilling sport as often as I can, and truly feel alive again!

# AROMATIC BBQ PORK RIBS

## WITH SPICY SLAW

Serves 6

## INGREDIENTS

**1lb pork belly bones in and skin on**

**1 cup of chicken stock**

BBQ SAUCE

**1 cup ketchup**

**1 cup Hoi sin sauce**

**2 tbsp Worcester sauce**

**2 tbsp soy sauce**

**1 tbsp ground 5 spice**

SPICY SLAW

**1 white onion sliced**

**1 cup of mayonnaise**

**¼ sliced white cabbage**

**2 large carrots peeled and grated**

**2 tbsp of Siracha**

## METHOD

Pre heat the oven to 300ºF/150ºC, salt the pork belly on a tray and add the chicken stock. Now place grease proof parchment on top before covering with foil. Put in the oven for 4 hours.

Mix all the ingredients for the BBQ sauce then set aside.

Mix all the ingredients for the spicy slaw then set aside.

Once the 4 hours are up, allow to cool and then add the left over stock to the BBQ sauce, putting as little fat in as possible. The skin should just pull off, if not use a knife to help. The idea is to have no fat or meat pulled off with the skin.

I like to make crackling with the skin but its does take time! To do so put the skin in a dry place for 24hrs, because if its not dry it wont bubble up. Then deep fry at 350ºC or more.

Cut into four pieces and then caramelize in a hot frying pan or on a smoking hot BBQ. It's important to really render that fat down, as it makes a huge difference on texture. Do so for about 2 minutes fat side down.

Dip each piece of pork in the BBQ sauce - literally submerge it, then place them on a tray with greaseproof paper.

Pre heat the oven to 400ºF/200ºC and roast for 20 minutes to give it a give a banging finish.

Serve with your spicy slaw and crackling!

# BBQ CHICKEN WINGS

## WITH LEMON, BLACK PEPPER AND PARMESAN WITH A SIDE OF SWEET

## CORN CHOWDER

Serves 4

## INGREDIENTS

1lb of organic chicken wings

4 tbsp grated parmesan

1 tsp black pepper

2 lemons zested and juiced

2 cartons of chicken bone broth

CHOWDER

1 tin of sweet corn

2 peeled garlic gloves pressed

1 onion finely diced

2 large potatoes, peeled and diced

1 leek, shredded (wash well)

Sliced spring onions

1 cup of double cream

1 cup of pancetta

## METHOD

Bring two liters of chicken stock to boil and then put all of the chowder ingredients in before adding the wings. Boil for 15 minutes, then remove the wings onto a paper towel.

Continue to simmer the chowder. Get the grill super hot and start to crisp up that skin. Grill until you have a nice golden char, then add the lemon, black pepper and parmesan.

Finish the chowder with cream and chopped spring onions and season.

# KING CRAB CAKES

## WITH LEMON AND GARLIC AIOLI

Serves 6

### INGREDIENTS

1 large egg

1 tbsp of Dijon mustard

3 tbsp mayonnaise

1 tbsp minced green onions

4 tsps lemon juice

1 tbsp chopped parsley

⅛ teaspoon red pepper flakes

8 ounces of cooked king crab (or tinned lump crab)

1 tbsp chickpea flour

½ cup breadcrumbs

Salt n pepper

Butter and olive oil to sauté

4 sprigs of thyme

LEMON AND GARLIC AIOLI

1 cup of olive oil

1 fresh egg

2 lemons juiced

2 raw peeled garlic cloves

1 tsp of salt

### METHOD

Mix all of the ingredients together, but don't over work the crab - we want large chunks. Then with your hands make 6 even balls and lightly press down to make a patty.

Put a non stick pan on medium heat, add the olive oil and butter, then start to caramelize the crab cakes. Flip over once there's a nice golden color. Add a little more butter and the thyme and start to baste. Set aside on a kitchen towel.

For the aioli, put all the ingredients into a toil measuring jug or container and emulsify with an emersion blender. Serve in a ramekin with the king crab cakes.

# KEY LIME PIE

## WITH SOFT MERINGUE

Serves 8

## INGREDIENTS

**300g speculoos ginger biscuits**

**110g melted butter**

**397g can condensed milk**

**3 medium egg yolks**

**3 medium egg whites**

**4 limes (finely grated zest, juiced)**

MERINGUE

**¼ cup icing sugar**

**3 medium egg whites**

**1 tsp cream of tartar**

## METHOD

Heat the oven to 320°F/160°C, and while that is pre heating whizz the biscuits into crumbs in a food processor.

Mix with the melted butter and press into the base and up the sides of a 22cm loose-based tart/pie tin.

Separate 3 medium eggs, put yolks in a large bowl and whisk for a minute. Add a can of condensed milk and whisk for another 2 minutes, then add the finely grated zest and juice of 4 limes and whisk again for 2 minutes.

Pour the filling into the cooled base then put back in the oven for 15 minutes. Allow to cool, then chill for at least 6 hours or overnight if you like. Carefully remove the pie from the tin and put on a serving plate.

Once you're ready to serve, whisk the egg whites until fluffy and smooth.

Then add the cream of tartar and continue whisking, adding the sugar a tablespoon at a time until soft peaks form. Place in a piping bag and decorate however you'd prefer! I like to cover in tear drops and then lightly blow torch to finish.  Or you can use a palate knife and lightly grill it for 30 seconds.

# MOM'S APPLE PIE

Serves 8

## INGREDIENTS

6-7 medium to large apples
(Granny Smith or Macintosh)

¾ cup sugar

¼ cup brown sugar

1 tbsp flour

1 tsp cinnamon

½ tsp nutmeg

1 tbsp butter

### PIE CRUST

3 cups flour

1 tbsp sugar

1 tsp salt

½ cup Crisco

½ cup (1 stick) cold butter

6-8 tbsp COLD water

## METHOD

To make the crust:
Combine the flour, sugar and salt in a bowl. Toss with a fork or by hand. With a pastry cutter, add in the butter and/or shortening until the mixture is crumbly.

Pour in ½ the water and mix well with a fork. Then add the remaining water in two stages, tossing flour mixture in between. You want your dough to be damp enough to work into a ball, but not too wet. You may not have to use all the water.

With floured hands, shape the dough into two balls, kneading slightly, but not over-working it. The one for the bottom crust should be slightly larger.

Flatten dough ball into a thick, round disk. Wrap in plastic wrap and put in the refrigerator for 30-45 minutes. This helps prevent sticking when you roll it out.

I sometimes skip that step, but then deal with sticky dough!

Flour the cutting board and rolling pin. Unwrap the dough and roll it out.

To make the pie:
Pre-heat the oven to 425°F/220°C. In a small bowl, combine the sugars, flour, cinnamon and nutmeg.

Peel, core and slice the apples into a large bowl. Toss with the sugar and spice mixture.

Fit the bottom crust into a 9-inch pie plate, preferable a heavy glass plate such as Pyrex.

Fill pastry-lined plate with the sugared apples. Press down on the apples with your hand or back of a spoon to reduce air pockets. Cute the tablespoons of butter into 3 or 4 pieces and dot the top of the apples. Cover the apples with the rolled-out top crust, trim the excess dough and crimp edges between thrumb and forefinger or the tines of a fork to seal the pie. With a sharp knife, cute 3-4 vent slits into the top of the pie.

Bake 50-60 minutes, or until the crust is golden brown. Enjoy!

*Chef's Note*

Recipe made with Pillsbury or Gold Medal unbleached, all-purpose flour. DO NOT USE self-rising flour. Also do not use butter-flavor Crisco unless a recipe specifically calls for it, and be sure not to use margarine or butter substitutes.

# WONDERFUL CHICKEN POT PIE

Serves 8

## INGREDIENTS

**1 cup diced peeled potatoes**

**¾ cup sliced carrots**

**½ cup (1 stick) butter, cubed**

**⅓ cup chopped onion**

**½ cup flour**

**1 tsp salt**

**½ tsp dried thyme**

**½ tsp pepper**

**1½ cups chicken broth**

**¾-1 cup milk**

**2 cups cooked chicken, cubed**

**1 package Pillsbury refrigerated pie crusts**

**Optional – ½ cup frozen peas**

## METHOD

To save time, you can buy pre-cooked un-breaded chicken strips typically found in the lunch meat aisle and chop them into chunks.

Pre-heat the oven to 425°F/220°C. In a large saucepan, bring carrots and potatoes to a boil. Reduce heat and simmer, covered until just tender, 8-10 minutes.

Drain.

In a large skillet, melt butter at medium-high heat and add the onion. Cook and stir until tender, only a few minutes.

Stir in flour and seasonings until blended, and then gradually add broth and milk. Cook and stir for 2 minutes or until thickened. Turn off heat. Stir in chicken, peas and potatoes.

Following package directions, unroll one pie crust and fit into pie plate. Add chicken mixture. Cover with top pie crust. Vent, seal and crimp.

Bake 35-40 minutes. Let stand 15 minutes before cutting.

# MALTA

## GRAND HARBOR

## FOR THE BELOW DECK MEDITERRANEAN FANS

This experience was both an incredible and exhausting journey, but life is always full of highs and lows. I made some amazing friends along the way and I'm very grateful for that! I wanted to include some recipes from my season as a tribute to the epic fans that supported me.

# PROTEIN PANCAKES WITH ITALIAN MERINGUE

## AND BLUEBERRIES

Serves 4

## INGREDIENTS

**50g vanilla protein powder**

**1 cup of oat flour**

**1 cup all-purpose flour**

**3½ teaspoons baking powder**

**1 tablespoon white sugar**

**¼ teaspoon salt, or more to taste**

**1¼ cups milk**

**3 tablespoons butter, melted**

**2 eggs**

ITALIAN MERINGUE

**1 cup sugar**

**½ cup water**

**4 large egg whites, at room temp**
**and preferably from fresh eggs**

**½ teaspoon cream of tartar**

## METHOD

Sift flour, oat flour, baking powder, sugar, and salt together in a large bowl. Make a well in the center and add milk, melted butter, protein powder, and eggs; mix until smooth.

Heat a lightly oiled griddle or pan over medium-high heat. Pour or scoop the batter onto the griddle, using approximately ¼ cup for each pancake. Cook until bubbles form and the edges are dry, about 2 to 3 minutes. Flip and cook until browned on the other side. Repeat with remaining batter.

MERINGUE

In a small saucepan, combine sugar and water. Heat over high heat, stirring only until it comes to a boil. Once it reaches a boil, stop stirring. Cook until sugar syrup registers 460°F/240°C on an instant-read or candy thermometer. Brush down sides of pot as necessary with a pastry brush dipped in water.

Meanwhile, combine egg whites and cream of tartar in the bowl of a stand mixer fitted with a whisk attachment. Set mixer to medium speed and mix until soft peaks form (when lifted, the head of the mixer should form gentle peaks in the egg whites that very slowly collapse back into themselves), about 2 minutes.

With the mixer running, carefully and slowly drizzle in hot sugar syrup. Increase speed to high and whip until desired stiffness is achieved. Soft peaks are often used to aerate mousses, for example, while a stiff peak is best for buttercream.

# SALT BAKED FISH

Serves 4

## INGREDIENTS

**2lb kosher salt**

**¾ cup water**

**1 - 2lb whole fish, such as bass, snapper, dorade, trout, or branzino, gutted**

**Lemon slices**

**Peeled garlic cloves**

**Peeled ginger slices, and/or fresh herb sprigs (such as parsley, dill, oregano, thyme, or tarragon), for stuffing**

## METHOD

Preheat oven to 400°F/200°C and set rack to middle position. Line a rimed baking sheet with parchment paper. In a large mixing bowl, stir together salt and water until thoroughly mixed and salt is damp but not soggy.

Stuff fish cavity with aromatics of your choice, then lightly brush olive oil all over the fish on both sides.

Spread about one-third of the salt mixture on the prepared baking sheet, covering an area just a little larger than the shape of the fish. Set fish on salt bed.

Fully cover the fish with the remaining salt, making sure to pack salt all around the fish in an even layer about ½ inch thick. Roast the fish, about 30 minutes for a 1-pound fish and 40 minutes for a 2-pound fish. Let rest 5 minutes.

Using a knife or a hammer, carefully cut into salt crust along the length of the fish on the side near its belly, then gently crack open salt to uncover fish. Being careful not to get the salt crust mixed into the flesh, remove and discard skin, then fillet the cooked fish and transfer to a platter. Serve.

*Chef's Note*

Make sure you leave the scales on the fish otherwise the flesh will become too salty!

# WHITE BREAD LOAF

Serves 6

*This was one of the loaves I would bake every morning. I had very little space and time so its perfect for anyone with a busy schedule, and its delicious!*

## INGREDIENTS

**1lb strong white bread flour**

**1½oz soft butter**

**7g sachet fast-action dried yeast**

**1½ tsp salt**

**10¾ fl oz tepid water**

**3 tbsp olive oil for the loaf tin**

## METHOD

Put the flour into a large mixing bowl and add the butter. Add the yeast at one side of the bowl and add the salt at the other, otherwise the salt will kill the yeast. Stir all the ingredients with a spoon to combine.

Add half of the water and turn the mixture round with your fingers. Continue to add water a little at a time, combining well, until you've picked up all of the flour from the sides of the bowl. You want the dough to be soggy, so continue to add the water.

Combine and use the mixture to clean the inside of the bowl. Keep going until the mixture forms soggy dough. If you have a KitchenAid use a dough hock and work for 2 minutes.

Clean and lightly oil the mixing bowl and put the dough back into it. Cover with a damp tea towel or lightly oiled cling film and set it aside to prove. This gives the yeast time to work: the dough should double in size. This should take around one hour, but will vary depending on the temperature of your room (don't put the bowl in a hot place or the yeast will work too quickly).

Put 3 tbsp of olive oil into a loaf tin. Once the dough has doubled in size scrape it out of the bowl, into the tin, and a place a damp cloth on top. Wait about 1.5 hours for the dough to double in size.

Preheat the oven to 425°F/220°C. Put an old, empty roasting tin into the bottom of the oven.

After an hour the loaf should have proved (risen again). Sprinkle some flour on top and very gently rub it in.

Put the loaf (on its baking tray) into the middle of the oven. Pour a little water into the empty roasting tray at the bottom of the oven just before you shut the door – this creates steam, which helps the loaf develop a crisp and shiny crust.

Bake the loaf for about 40 minutes. The loaf is cooked when it's risen and golden. To check, take it out of the oven and tap it gently underneath – it should sound hollow. Turn onto a wire rack to cool.

# PITA BREAD WITH TZATZIKI

Serves 6                    *From the Greek Lunch*

## INGREDIENTS

**Pita Bread**

**2 tsp fast-action dried yeast**

**500g strong white bread flour,**

**2 tsp salt**

**1 tbsp olive oil**

TZATZIKI

**½ cucumber, halved and deseeded**

**1 tbsp of chopped pickles**

**170g pot Greek yogurt**

**1 small garlic clove, crushed**

**Handful mint leaves, chopped**

**Handful of dill, chopped**

## METHOD

Coarsely grate the cucumber, sprinkle with a pinch of salt and squeeze out all the liquid. Tip into a bowl with the yogurt, garlic, dill, chopped pickles and mint, and mix well.

Mix the yeast with 300ml warm water in a large bowl. Leave to sit for 5 minutes until the yeast is super bubbly, then tip in the flour, salt and olive oil. Bring the mixture together into a soft dough. Don't worry if it looks a little rough round the edges.

Tip the dough onto a lightly floured work surface. Knead for 5-10 minutes until you have a soft, smooth and elastic dough. Try to knead using as little extra flour as possible, just enough so that the dough doesn't stick – this will keep the pittas light and airy. Once kneaded, place in a lightly oiled bowl, cover with a tea towel and leave to double in size, approximately 1 hour.

Heat oven to 350°F and put a large baking tray on the middle shelf of the oven to get searing hot. Divide the dough into eight balls and then flatten each into a disc with the palm of your hand. On a lightly floured surface, roll each disc into an oval, around 20cm long, 15cm wide and 3-5mm thick.

Carefully remove the hot tray from the oven. Dust with flour, then place the pittas directly onto it – you may have to do this in batches. Return swiftly to the oven and bake for 4-5 minutes. Once they are out use a blow torch on both sides to get a darker color and a charred flavor.

# MIRROR GLAZED VANILLA CAKE

## WITH STRAWBERRY JAM

Serves 12

*This is the same method I used to make all my cakes while I was on board, including the pink pearl and the green apples. Keep in mind this is a more complex process, but a lot of people have reached out asking how I did it.*

### INGREDIENTS

**50g butter, melted**

**250g plain flour**

**250g caster sugar plus 1 tbsp**

**5 medium eggs**

### BUTTER ICING

**250g soft butter**

**250g icing sugar**

**1 lemon zested**

### FOR THE CENTER

**200g icing sugar**

**1tbsp vanilla essence**

**250g cream cheese**

**1 jar strawberry jam**

### MIRROR GLAZE

**(the cheat and fast version)**

**2 tins of sweet condensed milk**

**6 gelatin leaves**

**Food coloring**

### FOR THE SPONGE

Heat oven to 375°F/190°C. Brush 2 x 20cm cake tins with melted butter, line the bases with baking paper, then dust well with flour tipping out any excess. Set aside.

Put the sugar and eggs in a large heatproof bowl, and then set it over a pan of barely simmering water. Whisk with an electric hand whisk for about 7 minutes or until the mixture is pale and has tripled in volume. Remove from the heat, then slowly pour in the butter folding it in as you pour until it is completely mixed in.

Gently fold the flour and a pinch of salt into the egg mixture, then pour into the prepared cake tins. Cook for 25 minutes until the cake is golden and risen – a skewer pushed into the cake should come out clean. Allow the cakes to cool for a few minutes in the tin, then remove and cool completely on a wire rack.

## FOR THE CENTER FILLING

For the center filling, whip all the ingredients in a KitchenAid or by hand, making sure there are no lumps. Set aside or put into a piping bag.

For the butter icing, put all the ingredients into the KitchenAid. Start slow and once the sugar has dissolved into the butter speed it up as we want to whip it hard to get as much air in as possible until it's a paler color. Put into a piping bag.

To assemble the cakes, cut each one in half horizontally. Put a cooling rack inside of a flat baking tray. Now place one sponge on top, spread a layer of jam, and then spread the cream mix on top. Place the other side on top and repeat. So now we have all 4 sides assembled. Pipe the butter icing, smothering the cake and leaving no gaps, then smooth out using a pallet knife. Place in the freezer for 1 hour.

For the mirror glaze put the gelatin leaves in cold water and wait until they are softened. Place into a medium sized pot with the sweet condensed milk, then put the pot on a very low heat. Continue to whisk until the gelatin dissolves ( do not turn the heat up as it will burn). After about 15 minutes pass the mix through a fine sieve, just to confirm the gelatin has dissolved. Split the glaze into two measuring jugs, leaving 80% in one and 20% in the other one. Then mix the blue food coloring in the bowl with 80% in. Now set aside and let it cool down to room temperature. Do not put it in the fridge.

Grab the cake out the freezer - it should be rock hard now. You want to scrape with the backside of your pallet knife to make the butter icing as smooth as possible, but bare in mind this is not easy. Then place back into the freezer.

Check the temperature of the glaze by using a thermometer – you're looking for about 60F. It will be like a thick double cream consistency.

Take the cake out of the freezer. Pour the white glaze slowly into the blue glaze, then pour over the top of the cake. Watch this beautiful pattern emerge between the two colors mixing as they glaze the cake! Place back in the freezer and wait for it to fully set.

This is definitely the hardest recipe to do in my book, so take your time and try your best! It's fun, messy and does take a little bit of time but you can really create some cool looking cakes with this method.

# SHISO LEAVES WITH SALMON AND SOUR PAPAYA

Serves 8

## INGREDIENTS

**Shiso leaves**

**6 slices sushi grade salmon**

**1 Sour Papaya**

### DRESSING

**1 tsp of diced ginger**

**1 tbsp shredded coriander**

**1 tbsp sesame oil**

**1 lime juiced**

**1 tbsp light soy sauce**

**Diced green chili for garnish**

## METHOD

Wash the shiso leaves in cold water, then let them dry off on a kitchen towel.

Use a peeler and take the skin off the papaya. It's much easier to leave it whole while you do this. With a mandolin, using the metal blade with the medium sized teeth, shred it to get a spaghetti-like finish. You can do it by hand too but using a mandolin is preferred

Put all the dressing ingredients into a blender and blitz until smooth. Once that's done, dress the papaya. Place the papaya onto the shiso, followed by the salmon, and garnish with the chili and a little drizzle of the excess dressing. So simple and so delicious. A great party snack with little time needed to prepare!

# EGGS BENEDICT

Serves 4

*I made A LOT of eggs benedict on the show, using my white bread loaf recipe instead of muffins, and it was a hit. I'll tell you one thing - if you can master the hollandaise sauce in the comfort of your own home it's very unlikely any restaurant will be able to beat it as it's rarely made to order.*

*It's amazing making it yourself because there's so many ways to customize this dish as well! Make it with pulled pork, beetroot cured salmon, truffle and caramelized mushrooms - the list is endless.*

## INGREDIENTS

**150g butter**

**3 egg yolks**

**½ tsp white wine vinegar**

**Squeeze of lemon juice**

**Pinch of cayenne pepper**

**1 egg**

## HOLLANDAISE SAUCE

Melt the butter in a saucepan and skim any white solids from the surface. Keep the butter warm.

Put the egg yolks, white wine vinegar, a pinch of salt and a splash of ice-cold water in a metal or glass bowl that will fit over a small pan. Whisk for a few minutes, then put the bowl over a pan of barely simmering water and whisk continuously until pale and thick, about 3-5 minutes.

Remove from the heat and slowly whisk in the melted butter bit by bit until it's all incorporated and you have a creamy hollandaise. (If it gets too thick, add a splash of water.) Now season with a squeeze of lemon juice and a little cayenne pepper. When serving it on top of eggs I love to gratinate it with a blow torch.

## SOUS VIDE EGG

The perfect temperature is 62.5°C and it must be cooked for 1 hour and 30 minutes. This will give you the perfect poached egg with a yolk that runs like butter.

Once the time is up, just crack the egg into boiling water with a little vinegar for 1 minute. This method will produce the best egg you've ever tasted! You'll need a water bath and a water thermostat, but a basic set should cost less than $100. If you're willing to give it a try I assure you it's worth it. This egg is so delicious it sits alone.

*Chef's Note*

Another great tip is to sous vide the eggs. What does that mean? Using a thermostat in a water bath and controling the temperature of the water. This is how I did it on the show. You just need to know the time and temperature, and I'll be sharing that with you here.

Life is messy sometimes, feels like your getting Peaed on. Ask for help, you're not alone!

# INDEX

# CONVERSION CHART

| CUPS | OZ | G | TBSP | TSP | ML |
|------|-----|-----|------|-----|-----|
| 1/16 | 1/2 | 15 | 1 | 3 | 15 |
| 1/8 | 1 | 50 | 2 | 6 | 50 |
| 1/4 | 2 | 60 | 4 | 12 | 60 |
| 1/3 | 3 | 70 | 5 | 16 | 70 |
| 1/2 | 4 | 115 | 8 | 24 | 125 |
| 2/3 | 5 | 140 | 11 | 32 | 150 |
| 3/4 | 6 | 170 | 12 | 36 | 175 |
| 1 | 8 | 225 | 16 | 48 | 250 |

| 250°F | 300°F | 325°F | 350°F | 400°F | 450°F |
|-------|-------|-------|-------|-------|-------|
| 120°C | 150°C | 160°C | 175°C | 200°C | 230°C |

In loving memory of Joe Harkess.
RIP brother, hope your cooking up a storm and shredding through some clouds.